WILD BRIGHT HOPE

Reflections on faith

THE BIG CHURCH READ LENT BOOK 2025

Published in Great Britain in 2024

SPCK
SPCK Group
Studio 101
The Record Hall
16–16A Baldwin's Gardens
London EC1N 7RJ

www.spckpublishing.co.uk

Copyright © SPCK 2024

The authors of the individual chapters included in this work have asserted their rights under the Copyright, Designs and Patents Act, 1988, to be identified as such.

All rights reserved. No part of this book may be reproduced or transmitted in any form or by any means, electronic or mechanical, including photocopying, recording, or by any information storage and retrieval system, without permission in writing from the publisher.

SPCK does not necessarily endorse the individual views contained in its publications.

British Library Cataloguing-in-Publication Data
A catalogue record for this book is available from the British Library

ISBN 978–0–281–09100–3
eBook ISBN 978–0–281–09101–0

1 3 5 7 9 10 8 6 4 2

Typeset by Fakenham Prepress Solutions, Fakenham, Norfolk NR21 8NL
First printed in Great Britain by Clays Limited, Bungay, Suffolk

eBook by Fakenham Prepress Solutions, Fakenham, Norfolk NR21 8NL

Produced on paper from sustainable sources

Contents

1	Seeds of unity: Alysia-Lara Ayonrinde	3
2	Reimagining day to day: Will Fremont-Brown	21
3	Kingdom, faiths and diplomacy: Cameron Howes	37
4	Wild paths of peace: Martha Jarvis	57
5	Hope and the Church of England: Cathrine Fungai Ngangira	77
6	A vision for hope in politics: Keziah Patterson	89
7	Widening horizons: Hannah Spiers	105
8	A beautiful and messy awakening: Belle Tindall	125
9	The radical grace of God: Toby Thomas	141
10	Good News, New Histories: Goodness Uwan-Owaji Victor	155
11	A journey through a supper table: Bhanuka Warnasooriya	163
12	Hope in suffering: Rachael Wooldridge	181
Notes		197

Acknowledgments

Scripture quotations marked ESV are from the ESV Bible (The Holy Bible, English Standard Version), copyright © 2001 by Crossway, a publishing ministry of Good News Publishers. Used by permission. All rights reserved.

Scriptures taken from Ikpa Mbuban The Bible in Obolo of Nigeria © 2012, The Nigeria Bible Translation Trust and Wycliffe Bible Translators, Inc. All rights reserved.

Scripture quotations marked NIV are taken from the Holy Bible, NEW INTERNATIONAL VERSION®, NIV®. Copyright © 1973, 1978, 1984, 2011 by Biblica, Inc.® Used by permission. All rights reserved worldwide.

Scripture quotations marked NRSV are taken from the New Revised Standard Version Bible, copyright 1989, Division of Christian Education of the National Council of the Churches of Christ in the United States of America. Used by permission. All rights reserved.

Scripture quotations marked NVI – PT are taken from Biblia Sagrada, Nova Versão Internacional®, NVI® Copyright © 1993, 2000 by Biblica, Inc.™ Used by permission. All rights reserved worldwide.

Scripture quotations marked NRSVuea are taken from the *New Revised Standard Version Bible Updated Edition*, British Text. Copyright © 2021 National Council of Churches of Christ in the United States of America. Used by permission. All rights reserved worldwide.

Page 134 'I Still Haven't Found What I'm Looking For' Lyrics © Polygram Int. Music Publishing B.V.

WILD BRIGHT HOPE

Alysia-Lara Ayonrinde is the Schools Project Lead for the Archbishop of Canterbury's Reconciliation Ministry. Her distinguished career in education spans over fifteen years, encompassing senior leadership roles across the UK, West Africa and South America. She brings unique, evidence-based perspectives that supportively challenge conventional norms to foster greater interfaith and intercultural understanding in schools, communities and churches.

Alysia-Lara is deeply committed to championing diversity, equity, inclusion and justice, evident through her transformative contributions to learning environments globally. She pioneers innovative strategies that empower leaders, teachers and students from all backgrounds to flourish.

Bible quotations in this chapter are taken from the NRSVA and the Portuguese Nova Versão Internacional (NVI-PT).

1
Seeds of unity

'Miss Ayonrinde, if you speak two languages the same [equally], what language do you dream in?'

A seven-year-old child asked me this question over fifteen years ago, and it has stayed with me ever since. At the time, I was reminded of my childhood and the blend of languages and cultures that shaped my hopes and dreams. It made me reflect on the language of the Holy Spirit – the deep, personal truths that are often revealed within us – and how we can lose sight of these amid clouds of doubt from the world around us.

Growing up, I struggled to express my faith. Elders in my family, fearing that talking freely at school or with friends might lead to misunderstanding or exclusion, advised me to keep my beliefs private. Their intention was to protect me, but what happened was that I became known as the 'quiet child' – not because I lacked things to say, but because I hid a significant part of who I was. Consider what it's like to be able to speak another language but to be too afraid to do so because of how others might respond. That's how I felt about sharing my faith and spirituality. This challenge became even greater after a traumatic loss during my childhood left me silent for several years.

The question from my young pupil reminded me of the importance of embracing one's identity. It highlighted the need for environments where children and young people can express their true selves without fear of being misunderstood or rejected. Recently, I had the privilege of speaking with twelve-year-old Patience from the Roma community, which often faces very high levels of discrimination and prejudice. She shared a perspective on belonging that touched my heart: 'Belonging means feeling comfortable and happy with who I am, and not having to mask with different people.'

The 'masking' that Patience mentioned demonstrates how children and young people can hide their expressions of faith in order to help others around them to feel comfortable. However, there are a multitude of ways in which Christianity is expressed across the world, and this creates a beautiful mosaic of traditions, practices and beliefs. Each of these expressions will be shaped by its context, the issues being grappled with and the people concerned. Research shows that 70% of Christians in the world are from Global Majority Heritage (GMH) backgrounds. Africa, for example, has over 650 million Christians. In fact, Nigeria has more Anglicans than North America and Europe put together.[1] This certainly challenges a typically Eurocentric view of the global religious landscape.

Children and young people in our churches, who are beginning to understand and appreciate such diversity, need to feel free to explore and articulate their faith in ways that make sense to them. This freedom is necessary not only for personal growth but to foster understanding and reconciliation within the broader Christian community.

A kingdom of many cultures

As Christians, we're called to embrace diversity in all its forms, including different worldviews that intersect with our faith. This is especially important in places such as Brazil, where – in some communities – indigenous beliefs and Christianity come together.

My own experience reflects this. Even though I was born and raised in the UK, my Brazilian and Nigerian heritage shaped my upbringing. My papa is Muslim, and my mama is indigenous Christian. Despite their different backgrounds and beliefs, there was a beautiful symbiosis between them, and we embraced the shared values that brought us closer, such as compassion, kindness and empathy.

I've often navigated between the traditions of my ancestors and the teachings of Christianity. The word 'syncretism' is used to describe how these can blend together. However, this term might oversimplify the way these beliefs mix. Particularly in the West, the cultural nuances of different beliefs coexisting and enhancing one another through shared values and experiences might not be fully understood.

In the vast tapestry of cultural and religious identities, few threads are as intricately woven as those in Brazil. For many indigenous communities around the world, Christianity was introduced through colonisation, often as a tool for conversion and assimilation. Instead of replacing indigenous beliefs, some communities included aspects of Christianity within existing spiritual practices that were distinct and deeply rooted in their cultural heritage.

To some, this might seem contradictory, but for those immersed in these traditions, it was not about choosing between belief systems but rather about finding harmony between them, honouring ancestral practices while embracing aspects of the Christian faith. In indigenous Brazilian communities, this practice permeates daily life, from the sacred use of plants to traditional festivals.

If you've seen the film *Avatar*, you might remember the heart-wrenching scene where Hometree is destroyed, and the Na'vis' anguished cries fill the air. Just as the Na'vis' bond with their environment reflects a sacred relationship, my tribe's commitment to nature stems from a deep, spiritual responsibility. This connection to the land is deeply rooted in our hearts and souls, guiding us to honour and protect the world we live in. However, understanding syncretism goes beyond simply acknowledging the coexistence of different beliefs; it's about recognising the strength and resilience of indigenous communities in the face of centuries of colonisation and oppression, and the ways in which they have preserved their culture.

I often meet people who describe this expression of Christianity as lacking authenticity or watering down the 'true faith'. This can be deeply hurtful – not just for me, but for many adults, children and young people whose cultures reflect diverse forms of Christianity. Celtic Christianity, which was influenced by pre-Christian beliefs and culture, might seem a more familiar example.

In any case, who gets to decide what is authentic? Authenticity isn't a fixed standard set by some; it's a lived experience shaped by the collective wisdom of indigenous communities. It's a way to keep cultural heritage alive while embracing the Christian faith, and a reminder that spirituality isn't limited to church buildings or specific doctrines but rather flows through the rivers, forests and mountains that have sustained our ancestors for generations.

Embracing diverse worldviews

In recent years, the term 'worldviews' has gained prominence, especially in religious education. For many people from Global Majority Heritage backgrounds, who interact with people of different cultures and faiths within their communities, contemplating the perspectives of others is nothing new.

One of the most beautiful aspects of embracing diverse Christian worldviews is recognising that every person is made in the image of God. Psalm 139:14 says, *'Eu te louvo porque me fizeste de modo especial e admirável. Tuas obras são maravilhosas! Digo isso com convicção.'* This verse reminds us that we are 'fearfully and wonderfully made' by God and celebrates the uniqueness and intrinsic value of each individual. Understanding that we are all created in God's image encourages us to appreciate the diverse ways in which people experience and express their faith. It's a powerful reminder that our differences are not flaws but part of God's marvellous design. Consider the example of pineapple on pizza – a serious no-go for me but for some a culinary delight! As the Nigerian-born author Ola Joseph said, 'Diversity is not about how we differ. Diversity is about embracing one another's uniqueness,'[2] and therefore seeing the humanity in others.

As Christians, this isn't just about theological dialogue; it's about embodying Christ's love in a world where many hunger for acceptance and reconciliation.

Reflection questions

1 How can I better appreciate and respect the different expressions of Christianity in my community?
2 What misconceptions or stereotypes might I hold, and how can I challenge and change them?
3 How can I practise cultural humility to celebrate and learn from the diverse Christian practices of others?

Bridging faith and cultures in a modern world

When I was a deputy headteacher, I told a class of nine- to eleven-year-olds a story about the experience of Liliana, an eight-year-old child at school in the UK. Liliana learned about the terrible loss of marine life due to the Deepwater Horizon oil spill in the Gulf of Mexico (which occurred in 2010), and she was inconsolable, unable to articulate her grief. When her mum arrived, the teacher expressed surprise at the child's 'extreme reaction'. Her mother explained that the family's faith and culture emphasised a deep connection with nature, inspired by their belief in God as the Creator of all things. For Liliana, this wasn't just an environmental disaster; it was a personal and spiritual crisis.

After hearing the story, a child in my own class began to cry. She came from a farming community. During lambing season, when each lamb's survival is crucial, the death of even one would be felt deeply by this young girl. The shared experiences of these two children highlight the universal themes of stewardship and the human–nature relationship across different cultures and communities, all viewed through the lens of Christian faith. It shows us that there is more that unites us than divides us.

Uchimura Kanzō, a Japanese author and a Christian, believed that the entire world could be seen as a place of prayer. For him, the church was not just a building but the whole of creation, from the sun that shines in the sky to the stars that sparkle at night. Despite geographical distances and cultural differences, children and young people can share a natural curiosity and sensitivity to the world around them and a deep sense of responsibility to care for it.

Lessons from lived experiences

You might be wondering why I've chosen to focus on children and young people in my chapter, especially when aspects of global Christianity might seem too complex for them (and us) to grasp. The reason is that children and young people are at a crucial stage in their lives, forming their beliefs, values and sense of identity. The stories we tell them hold incredible power in shaping these aspects. They can make complex ideas more accessible, planting seeds of hope and guiding young minds as they grow into compassionate and informed individuals.

We can reflect on the stories we are telling in our contexts.

- How do we tell them?
- Who's holding the pen?
- Whose voices are missing?
- Do the stories we tell empower and humanise others?

Practically, this translates into sharing diverse stories and perspectives. However, it also requires us to set aside time for children, young people and adults to share their experiences and listen to the stories of others – particularly those from marginalised communities – with openness, respect and empathy.

In my work and beyond, I am privileged to hear the stories and questions of children and young people, and these often reveal incredible insights and truths. Recently, a thirteen-year-old asked, 'What do you do when your saviour and oppressor have the same face?' Let's pause and reflect on this for a moment.

The question encapsulates the deep struggle many people face in reconciling their faith with historical and contemporary injustices. Two years ago, I learned about the Slave Bible for the first time. The Slave Bible, formally titled *Parts of the Holy Bible, Selected for the Use of the Negro Slaves, in the British West-India Islands*, was published in 1807. It was a heavily edited version of the Bible used by British missionaries to convert enslaved Africans to Christianity. Crucial portions, including the story of the Israelites' exodus from Egypt and any passages that promoted freedom or justice, were removed. The purpose was to prevent enslaved people from getting ideas about liberation or rebellion. The Slave Bible focused instead on passages that promoted obedience and submission.

When I discovered that a copy of this volume was held by the very institution I worked for, I had to confront a particularly stark instance of how Christianity had been weaponised, and it caused me to experience spiritual trauma. The Bible, which I had always seen as a source of hope and guidance, had been used to justify and perpetuate oppression. So, when the thirteen-year-old asked, 'What do you do when your saviour and oppressor have the same face?', I empathised deeply with her struggle to understand such a dark aspect of history. How could a faith, meant to bring light and love, be twisted into a tool of control and oppression? It was a painful question. Yet, in the midst of what was being revealed, there was hope.

The concept of *kintsugi*, the Japanese art of repairing broken pottery with gold, teaches us that beauty and strength can emerge from brokenness. Recognising the dark parts of our history allows us to address and learn from them. We cannot have reconciliation without the truth. By confronting these truths, we can work towards more inclusive and compassionate expressions of Christianity, ensuring that such manipulation never happens again. We can reframe our faith in a way that aligns with its true teachings of love, justice and equality. Although this might be difficult, it is necessary for healing and growth.

Professor Paul Miller,[3] in teaching about how to listen to children and young people, inspires us to do so without interruption and judgement but with discernment. When we listen without interruption, we create a safe environment where every voice feels valued. When we listen without judgement, we create a culture and space of empathy, allowing young people to express their truths without fear of rejection. When we listen with discernment, we ensure that those who might struggle to articulate their thoughts clearly, or those who might not be as loud as others, are still heard and understood. Lastly, we can listen without the need to hear words, simply cherishing every individual's uniqueness.

Our children and young people today do not see matters of reconciliation, faith and identity as optional or a phase they're going through, but as utterly necessary, especially in an age when social media consistently reminds us that we're living through turbulent times. If we are intentional about listening and responding to them from a very young age, voicing their views and being involved will become normal for teens and young adults. There is a significant difference between consultation and genuine participation, and it's exciting to think that such a change is possible.

Reflection questions

1 How can I listen to children and young people without interruption or judgement, making sure that they feel safe and valued when they share their thoughts and feelings about their faith?
2 How can I create an environment where young people feel understood and supported in their faith journey,

especially when they face complex issues like reconciling faith with historical and contemporary injustices?
3 How can I ensure that young people's voices are not only heard but also allowed to influence the way we practise and understand Christianity together?

When do you see or experience God?

When we consider the importance of community, especially for children and young people, understanding where they see or experience the presence of God is crucial. Community, rooted in belonging and togetherness, takes on new dimensions when we consider global Christianity. By exploring diverse geographic, historical and cultural contexts, we gain insights into how these factors shape Christian experiences and beliefs around the world.

Here are some reflections from children and young people on how they've perceived the presence of God.

Five-year-old from Italy 'I see God when I look at the stars with my mummy. They are so pretty and make me feel like God is watching over us.'

Seven-year-old from India 'I see God when I light a candle with my parents. The warm glow makes me feel like God is close to me.'

Eight-year-old from Brazil 'I feel God's presence when we dance and sing in our church during festivals. It feels like God's joy is all around us.'

Seeds of unity

Ten-year-old from Kenya 'I experience God when I help my friends at school. Sharing with others makes me feel God's love inside me.'

Ten-year-old from the UK 'I experience God when I am with my nana. She teaches me about God whenever she talks to me. For example, to treasure the life I have and not waste it, and to be grateful to God for the life he gave me.'

Eleven-year-old from Japan 'I see God when I meditate in the garden, listening to the birds and the wind. It feels peaceful, like God is whispering to me through nature.'

Twelve-year-old from Canada 'I feel God's presence when I volunteer at the local shelter. Helping others reminds me of God's kindness.'

Thirteen-year-old from Nigeria 'I see God when we gather as a family to pray every evening. Our prayers bring us closer to God and to each other.'

Fourteen-year-old from Australia 'I feel God's presence when I surf. Being in the ocean, feeling the power of the waves, reminds me of how big and strong God is.'

Fifteen-year-old from Iran 'I feel God's presence when I'm dealing with confusion or making tough decisions. When I pray or talk to someone I trust about my worries, it reminds me that God is guiding me through the confusion.'

Seeds of unity

Sixteen-year-old from Germany 'I experience God when I play music. The melodies and harmonies make me feel connected to something bigger than myself.'

Seventeen-year-old from Mexico 'I see God when we celebrate *Día de los Muertos*. Honouring our ancestors and feeling their presence makes me feel connected to God's eternal love.'

Eighteen-year-old from South Africa 'I feel God's presence during community service projects. Building homes or planting trees with others makes me feel like we are doing God's work together.'

Eighteen-year-old from the UK 'I feel the presence of God when I learn about global issues such as climate change or social justice. Working on these problems, whether through advocacy, volunteering or raising awareness, helps me care for others and the world. It helps me understand how faith can drive positive change in the world.'

Each young person's expression of where they see or experience God's presence – whether through nature, dance, family, church, school, personal reflections or global issues – is unique. Engaging with their voices helps us to better understand them and offers us a glimpse of the ways God is working in their lives. This approach aligns with Christ's teachings to care for and listen to the youngest members of our communities, nurturing their hopes and guiding them as they grow in faith.

Understanding global Christianity: A foundation for reconciliation

Imagine a child standing at the crossroads of cultures, with a heart that appreciates the many ways in which people practise their faith around the world. Picture young minds not limited by narrow views but enriched by the diverse tapestry of global Christianity. This isn't just a nice idea; it's crucial for creating a more harmonious world. The foundation of reconciliation is compassion and understanding, and it's this – especially among our children and young people – that will help to heal the divides between us.

Let's tell children and young people stories from around the globe, especially from indigenous and marginalised communities whose voices are often left unheard. Let's immerse them in art, music and traditions from various cultures, so they can experience the beauty and diversity within Christianity.

Creating opportunities for dialogue is also vital. Setting up discussion groups where children and young people can interact respectfully with peers from different cultural backgrounds helps them to develop understanding and builds bridges of unity. Celebrating global Christian festivals – perhaps exploring how Easter is celebrated in different countries or learning about unique events like the Ethiopian Timkat or aerial kites in Bermuda – makes the global Christian community tangible and meaningful.

Young people who have learned to value and respect diverse Christian faith expressions are more likely to approach conflicts with open minds and compassionate hearts. They will be better prepared to challenge prejudice, stand up for justice and work towards the common good. These young ambassadors of reconciliation will embody love, acceptance and unity. As they grow and take on leadership roles, their influence can shape cultural narratives and inspire others to embrace inclusivity. Although the journey might be long and challenging, the promise of a reconciled world makes every step worth it.

When we invite children and young people to, 'Come as you are and be included,' we acknowledge the strength in their vulnerability. We need to surround them with a circle of compassion, so they can experience true belonging and simply be themselves.

Reflecting on this, I recall how my grandmother used to ask me, 'What made your heart sing today?' This simple question was her way of encouraging me to reflect on the positive aspects of my day and recognise the joy in my experiences. Similarly, when we engage with children and young people, asking them about what inspires or moves them can help us to understand their unique perspectives, and it enables a deeper connection with their experiences.

Let's revisit the question posed by my young pupil at the beginning of this chapter: 'Miss Ayonrinde, if you speak two languages the same [equally], what language do you dream in?' Although I struggled to answer at the time, I now believe that we dream in the language of hope. Hope is the heartbeat of the soul. Through Christ, we can envision a brighter future where people from every nation, tribe and tongue unite. Hope fuels our deepest aspirations and drives us towards a world transformed by faith, love and reconciliation where unity and understanding prevail.

Will Fremont-Brown is the Church of England's Public Policy Advisor on Economics and Social Welfare, supporting and advising the archbishops, bishops and General Synod on issues relating to poverty, social security and strengthening communities across urban and rural contexts. He previously managed the Secretariat of the Archbishops' Commissions.

2

Reimagining day to day

During a cold week in January 2023, I had two very different appointments in my diary as part of my work on the Archbishops' Reimagining Care Commission. On Tuesday, I visited a community centre in South London. They were hosting activities for everyone in the community with a particular focus on people with learning disabilities, autism and mental health support needs. The centre was buzzing from the moment its doors opened at ten o'clock. Around thirty people came and went over the course of a few hours. Some made paper aeroplanes, which were launched around the hall with enthusiasm – if not always with accuracy. Others painted, crafted and knitted. Almost everyone took part in the musical arrangement featuring a large bongo and a wooden percussion frog, a joyful noise filling the space. A little black and white dog, which seemed to belong to everyone, waddled up and down greeting people as they arrived. Over a cup of tea, one of the regular attendees quietly told me that it was her birthday. Although she did not want a fuss to be made, it was lovely to see her face light up when others overheard and started to make one. I left the centre feeling energised, with the sound of the percussion frog croaking in my ears.

On Thursday, I travelled about three miles down the road from the community centre to the Houses of Parliament.

I was accompanying members of the Reimagining Care Commission to several meetings with politicians, including the government minister responsible for social care in England. Fresh from our time at the community centre (some of the other members had visited too), we carried with us the buzz from the room, the warmth of the fellowship, and most of all the sense that we were all welcomed and included no matter who we were, where we had come from or why we were there. As we spoke to politicians and leaders, we shared these impressions, making the point that we had not seen anything revolutionary. In fact, there were probably similar activities going on in community centres and church halls up and down the country on the same day to ensure that people had somewhere warm to be, alongside friends and neighbours, in a place where they would be noticed and cherished. We were aiming to bridge the gap between the reality of people's lives and the decisions taken in Westminster that affected them. We were trying to move the conversation away from the language of constraint to that of possibility.

I hope that the activities of this one week in January give you a flavour of the exciting approach taken by the three commissions established by the archbishops of Canterbury and York. They were set up as an opportunity to dig deeper into the subject areas explored by Archbishop Justin Welby in his book *Reimagining Britain*, in which he argued that we need a better story to tell about our country and a shared set of values and priorities around which to coalesce. The first edition, published in 2018, was written during the polarising debate about Brexit.

Reimagining day to day

The second edition, published in 2021, came out in the middle of a global pandemic that upended just about every area of life. *Reimagining Britain* invited readers to explore different areas of public life through the lens of Christian theology, tradition and values. With the gift of time, the commissions dug deeper into some of the challenges facing our communities and country and thought creatively about a future in which everyone can flourish.

- The Archbishops' Commission on Housing, Church and Community (2019–2021) looked at housing in the context of a crisis in which too many people do not have a safe, affordable, decent place to call home.
- The Archbishops' Commission on Reimagining Care (2021–2023) focused on adult social care and what is needed to support older people and disabled people to live well.
- The Archbishops' Commission on Families and Households (2021–2023) explored the ways families and households, in all their diversity, could be supported and strengthened.

The archbishops appointed members to the commissions who had professional expertise across a range of subject areas for the tasks of listening, conferring and proposing recommendations. It soon became apparent that members' life experiences would also be important. For example, when the Reimagining Care Commission met for the first time, we all had a personal story to share about caring for loved ones or drawing on care and support ourselves. This blend of expertise and experience was valuable and made for fascinating conversations. I found it a real privilege to work alongside the commissions on Families and Households and Reimagining Care to help them to report back to the archbishops and wider Church on their findings.

The process of reimagining

In his speech at the launch event of the Families and Households Commission, Archbishop Justin noted that the task of reimagining was about moving beyond what *is* towards what *could be* if we worked together, articulated shared values and lifted our eyes and aspirations. As I worked on the commissions, I got used to starting from a hopeful place. We began not with the challenges that so often shape our debates on important social issues but by spending time alongside people and finding out what life is like for them. We gathered stories through a comprehensive process of listening and engagement, inviting people to send us their ideas of places to visit, information on projects they had seen make a difference and suggestions on how we could reimagine together. So many people have stories to tell that can increase our sense of empathy, enrich our political discourse and improve our leaders' ability to make informed decisions. But people with these stories rarely feature in policy documents and reports, never mind in the rooms where important decisions are made. From the start, the commissions sought to change this as far as possible.

Reimagining day to day

None of the commissions started out with the belief that this work alone could reimagine these difficult policy areas. Rather, they identified that the Church has a distinctive role to play in contributing towards a reimagined future, which requires collective endeavour and an enduring commitment to change from across society. Christians have long been involved in the process of reshaping our society and contributing to lasting social reforms, from the abolition of the slave trade to the creation of the welfare state. Our tradition reminds us of the way that the Church, at its best, can be part of change. Today, if you visit any parish, you will find different ways in which the clergy and congregation express their calling to love God and live out the good news in supporting others. During the course of our work, we met with three mothers who were part of the Springfield Project, a Christian charity in Birmingham that runs a programme of community activities aiming to empower, enable and enrich the lives of local children, young people and families. The three mothers we met spoke about how the support they received had increased their confidence, self-esteem and well-being. One said, 'I usually stay at home or just do a bit of shopping. Now I look forward to coming here because I've made new friends, and it lifts my mood.' We also met with family carers from different religious traditions as part of an online gathering convened by the charity Carers UK. Without shying away from the difficulties that can come from caring for a loved one at home, they spoke movingly about the source of strength they find in their faith and community. When we visited MHA Moor Allerton, a retirement home in Leeds, we heard about the importance of taking the spiritual needs of residents seriously through the provision of inclusive worship and pastoral care. As people live longer, these efforts will be particularly important within churches and care homes.

Of course, not everything we encountered was positive, and we heard concerns too. Is reimagining too idealistic, too woolly, too unrealistic? How can we talk about reimagining the future of housing or social care when, right now, we cannot even get the basics right? We met with single people who expressed frustration that the Church had not always been a place where they felt embraced and valued. We heard from people in overcrowded accommodation who had little prospect of finding anywhere with enough space to live comfortably together. We met parents of disabled adults who told us about sleepless nights worrying about what would happen to their children once they were no longer around to care for them. In these moments, a concept like reimagining does not always feel like the most practical response. It might seem like a good idea for those with the privilege of a comfortable home, access to care if they need it and stable family lives. But those in the middle of a crisis probably do not have time to wait for a shiny new report to make recommendations that might not be enacted until well into the future. It was important that we heard these concerns and took them seriously. As we did so, we remembered that the task of reimagining needs to be undertaken in the knowledge of who we are and what we believe as followers of Jesus Christ.

The place of hope

Fundamentally, reimagining must begin with a shared commitment to hope. Hope in the Christian sense is not the same as optimism – the belief that, having assessed the evidence, a positive change is coming. Rather, hope is the certain assurance that God is faithful to his promises and will deliver for his people even when, outwardly, there is no evidence that anything is going to change for the better. Our hope enables us to persevere as we remember that God – mysteriously, wonderfully, unstoppably – is in the process of transforming the world. In the context of deeply complex social problems all around us, the Church must hold on to hope. Moreover, responding to God's love enables us not only to point towards a hopeful future but to embody hope in the way we live now. The love of God, revealed to us through the life, death and resurrection of Jesus Christ, defines who we are, transforms us completely and empowers us to love one another just as God has first loved us. The task for us, then, is to share and embody God's love in a world longing for hope, grace and transformation.

Clearly this is not a straightforward task. Indeed, reimagining requires repentance. In the first words he speaks in Mark's Gospel, Jesus calls on the people to turn around and reorientate their lives towards him. As we look at the world, we cannot help but recognise our own failure to hold power to account. We might even see ways in which we perpetuate inequality and injustice through our own decisions and lifestyle choices. But as we repent, we are invited into a new relationship that requires our participation. We are not called simply to receive the blessings of God's kingdom but to live radically different, hopeful lives.

The commissions' findings

Reflecting on what they had seen and the people they had met over the course of two years, each commission produced a report with recommendations for the Church of England, the Government and wider society about what it would take to reimagine the issue they had examined.

Whether in housing, social care or family life, all three called for a new commitment to putting values at the heart of a reimagined vision.

The Housing, Church and Community Commission argued that good housing must meet five basic tests:

1 It must be *safe*, prioritising the security of every single person living within the home.
2 It must be *sustainable*, not undermining the planet but working in harmony with the natural environment.
3 It must be *stable*, enabling people to stay and put down roots.
4 It must be *sociable*, designed in such a way that we can enjoy being in the space and offer hospitality to others.
5 It must be *satisfying*, a place in which we want to spend time.

The Reimagining Care Commission outlined a different way of thinking about, organising and delivering social care. As its main recommendation, the commission called on the government to establish a National Care Covenant. The purpose of this covenant would be threefold:

1 It would create a process through which people could feed in their views and ideas, so the Government could hear from people most affected by the current crisis.
2 It would be the means of setting out mutual responsibilities, clarifying what is expected of individuals, families and communities alongside local and national government.
3 It would indicate that social care is, by definition, relational and cannot be reduced to a series of contracts when it is fundamentally about how we relate to – and care for – one another.

The Families and Households Commission set out five key messages, stating that society should:

1 Value families in all their diversity, meeting their basic needs by putting their well-being at the heart of government policymaking and our community life, including religious communities.
2 Support relationships throughout life, ensuring that everyone is able to develop and maintain loving and caring relationships, manage conflict well and promote the flourishing of individuals and families.
3 Honour singleness and single-person households, recognising that loving relationships matter to everyone.
4 Empower children and young people, developing their

relational skills and knowledge, recognising their value and agency, protecting them from harm and giving them the best start in life.
5 Build a kinder, fairer and more forgiving society, removing discrimination, division and deep inequality for the sake of every family and household.

As we sought to propose new policies and solutions, we argued that the right values are not currently in place. This lack is often starkly revealed in policies and systems that do not honour the dignity and worth of every person. If we recognised the inherent and equal worth of every single child, we would not persist with a policy that restricts the financial support given to a household through Universal Credit to the first two children. If we believed that everyone should have a roof over their heads, we would tackle rough sleeping with the same energy and endeavour as we did at the start of the Covid-19 pandemic. If we treated social care with the same importance as healthcare, we would have a system that meets people's physical and emotional needs. Having consulted with a wide range of people and communities about the values that lie at the heart of reimagining, the commissions argued that embedding these in our practices would have a lasting impact.

In essence, reimagining depends on partnership. This is partly practical, because without a commitment to partnership, the changes the commissions called for would receive neither backing from across the political spectrum nor the participation of communities and agencies with the means of delivering for people in their local context.

Without a sense of collective purpose, any changes could easily be reversed. Meaningful change requires some level of consensus across society about core values and a commitment to bringing these to life. But the need for partnership is not primarily about expediency. In 1 Corinthians 12, Paul writes that we must work together in order to fulfil our calling as the body of Christ, one part as the hand, another the eye and another the foot. As we reimagine a different future, we commit to the kind of partnership that affirms our mutual dependence. The choice of each commission to establish partnership at the heart of their proposals reflects their response to God's call that we *all* play a part in contributing to our common life together.

Where do we go from here?

In the face of such complex issues, how will we know if we are reimagining housing, social care and family life along the lines set out by the commissions?

I think the fact that *reimagining* is an active verb is a clue that there is no final destination. Reimagining will be an ongoing process that requires the active participation of each of us as we listen, understand and partner together in the pursuit of change. But as we do this, I believe that we can expect to see some fruit from our labour.

Through the Reimagining Care Commission, the charity Livability (now Shaftesbury) invited us to a conversation with members of their Changes for the Future Forum, which brings together adults with a variety of disabilities to have a say in the way their services are delivered. The stories they shared had such an impact on us that we invited them to the report launch event to share their experiences with a wider audience.

Tom told us how important it is to include people who draw on care in these conversations so they are listened to and empowered. Debbie spoke about how her support worker enables her to live the life she wants to lead, going to church and sharing her faith, working at McDonald's and volunteering with St John Ambulance so she can help other people. Sharon and Michelle exchanged stories of discos and birthday parties at their care home and how much they valued the support they had received to pay their respects to Her Late Majesty Queen Elizabeth II during her lying-in-state. They all reflected on the difference it made to be part of a group where they were treated as valued partners with perspectives that would improve their care and the care given to others.

The Housing, Church and Community Commission saw examples of churches rolling up their sleeves and making a difference in their local communities. St Silas Church in Blackburn worked with a local charity to convert their church hall into purpose-built accommodation for homeless teenagers, offering them a pathway from the streets towards permanent accommodation of their own. Churches in Ealing came together and successfully persuaded candidates in their local elections to commit to requiring developers to provide 50% affordable housing on all new developments in the borough. In the Lake District, where tourism and second homes have driven up market rents, Keswick Churches Together formed their Community Housing Trust and developed homes on unused land, a number of which are let out at affordable rents as defined in relation to local earnings. These are all tangible signs of change at work and new foundations being laid for the future.

The Families and Households Commission saw some of the fruit of reimagining as it engaged with children and young people across the country. Most of the visits and video calls we had were with church youth groups, but others were organised through schools. Students at Gosport and Fareham Multi-Academy Trust, which several members of the commission visited, put together a package of resources after the commission's work finished, taking the initiative to create space for their peers to think through some of the big questions about relationships and identity as they prepared to leave home and make their own choices. We had the privilege of hearing from a number of young people at our launch event and drew hope from their mature reflections on the nature of family life.

I wonder how we could lean into the concept of reimagining as communities of Christians in a whole host of different areas. How might a church, sensing a renewed calling to engage with the world around them, discern what is theirs to do? Perhaps they could set up a community café, or make an unused piece of land the church owns available for the development of affordable homes, or redevelop the church's sanctuary so everyone has physical access to the space without any barriers. As we reimagine, may we be inspired – and inspire others – to look at our communities afresh, to think differently and to try something new, all for the glory of God.

In many cases, the results of reimagining might not be easy to see. There is no key performance indicator to monitor how many people know the name of their next-door neighbour. There is no way of measuring the deep sense of satisfaction when a family enjoys a meal together on a Sunday afternoon, or how a person who previously felt lonely finds companionship by taking part in a new activity club. But these fruits are expressed through restored relationships that reflect God's love. The vast majority of the projects we visited are still running several years after the commissions finished their work. The community centre where we saw such joy and purpose still offers activities that enable people to do the things they love with others. Often, these initiatives are not a means to an end but an expression of God's kingdom taking root all around us.

Reimagining: a collective effort

Despite the dedicated work of the people in all three commissions, each of the topics explored requires more time, energy and attention. The commissions were never designed to solve all the issues they confronted but rather to shine a light and create space for creative thinking. Our shared hope is that each of the reports developed by these commissions brought us deeper into the process of reimagining and, perhaps, closer to bearing some fruit. They reminded us about the importance of community and living out our faith by expressing our commitment to the flourishing of every single person. We will only know with time whether we are travelling in the right direction, but our shared commitment feels like a very good place to start.

As the commissions sought to demonstrate, reimagining requires us to favour the views and voices of people who are often ignored. We are called to seek out, celebrate and give the seat of honour at the table to those who have been forgotten, undermined and excluded for too long. After all, we follow the one who lavished his love upon the disheartened and dispossessed.

Churches have a central role to play in the reimagining process. We have people who seek to love their neighbour and serve their community. We have physical spaces within communities where people can come and share in common life together. We have a prophetic calling to embody hope. The fruits of reimagining might be slow in coming. Indeed, we might give everything we have and still fall short of our aspirations. But embodying hope requires us to trust in God's promise of renewal and restoration, when all things will be made new. We are invited to play our part. How might we join in? Where will we start?

Reflection questions

1 What might reimagining look like in your area?
2 Where do you see signs of hope in your church or faith community?
3 How could you get involved with different projects and activities taking place in your neighbourhood?

Cameron Howes is a Senior International Policy Adviser at the British Academy. Prior to that, he worked as a researcher and dialogue practitioner at the LSE Religion and Global Society research unit on interfaith and cross-cultural engagement, and policy for grassroots communities and government within the UK and internationally. Cameron holds an MSc in social psychology from the LSE specialising in religious cognition.

Bible quotations in this chapter are taken from the NRSVue and NRSV.

3

Kingdom, faiths and diplomacy

Usually, looking to the east on a winter morning ignites the soul. There is a beautiful intensity to the contrast of feeling the chill of winter at your back and being embraced by the warmth of God's healing light as the sun shines on your face.[1] But this particular winter dawn in East Jerusalem was different for me. Blocking out the sun's warming rays and casting a shadow that extended intrusively and well beyond the boundaries of the perimeter road was a nine-metre-high concrete wall. When viewed from the historic Mount of Olives, the snaking grey barrier seemed to blend into the arid landscape, but up close, it dwarfed its surroundings and cut awkwardly through small mounds deemed too insignificant to flatten – or indeed to name. I was not alone on that chilling morning. In the shadow of this icon of separation, I stood shoulder to shoulder with young Jews, Muslims and Christians from a variety of denominations.

Shoulder to shoulder in the shadows

We had been brought together by a university interfaith programme that sought to foster constructive engagement with the Israel–Palestine conflict among students from diverse religious and political perspectives. Having spent weeks preparing as a group to build trust in – and understanding of – one another, this was the first material test of how far that emerging solidarity would stretch.

Walls are not just physical objects; they signify and embody something acutely political. In our group, this wall evoked feelings of anger, protection, exclusion, relief, grief, curiosity and longing. Yet we were moved to a shared silence, the only response that felt appropriate when directly confronted with such unmistakable evidence of human failure.

I'm not ignorant to the litany of human tragedies and evils that have led us to this point. But in a book about hope, it feels important to start with a symbol of defeat, perhaps even the apparent death of hope. For me, the erection of the wall represents the conscious choice to give up on a divinely endorsed common life in favour of a common lie: that separation is safety, and partition is peace.

Kingdom diplomacy within the common life

I'm a bit of a curiosity. Growing up in an area of London with a large South Asian community, my best friends at primary school were a Muslim, a Jain and a Sikh. My lived experience of my neighbours has never mapped onto the more divisive rhetoric we are exposed to, which is often informed by fear and ignorance. I was a history and politics student during the Brexit referendum and felt deeply concerned by the community rifts that were magnified by our polarising politics. I was drawn to events and activities that tried to bring communities together in healing, and I wanted to do this through my primary identity: my Christian faith. Very quickly I learned how much connection could be made across faith identities and belief systems through interfaith work, and I have never looked back.

You might have been to an interfaith event in your local community – perhaps a coffee morning at your local church where scones have been substituted for samosas and cake for challah. Perhaps you've worked together across communities at your local food bank, an open memorial service or an event marking Remembrance Day. Such acts of hospitality might feel marginal, yet they are of global significance. In an age of instantaneous information, the way people of faith treat their neighbours in one part of the world has profound implications for religious communities and their local relationships everywhere – something we are living out very vividly in the wake of 7 October 2023.

Over the past decade, I have centred my community work and academic research on interfaith engagement, most of it at the LSE Faith Centre.[2] The centre was founded in 2014 to promote interreligious understanding across people of all faiths and none and to foster a new generation of interfaith peacebuilders. It does this through academic research, student programmes and international engagements (more on this later). Throughout my time at the centre, I have become primarily concerned with three deceptively simple questions:

1 What is interfaith engagement for?
2 What prevents people from engaging across religious differences?
3 How can interfaith engagement be fostered effectively?

I want to draw you into considering these questions by telling you about what I have experienced both professionally and as an Anglican. Perhaps you will also be challenged to consider what it really looks like to live with hope in a divided society.

Interfaith engagement is an expression of the obligations we all hold. Christians are not only called to a common life with one another but *the* common life with all creation. The common life is a form of radical interdependence that demands the full acknowledgement of our differences in order to enact the covenantal commitment to love as we are loved. It is not sameness. Not always, but very often, we perceive similarity because we are not paying real attention. We are called to see people as they are, as God sees them, and not as neat projections that suit our narrative. This is the cornerstone of our participation in the building of God's kingdom.

While we can appreciate this heavenly calling, our world constructs barriers. The fact is that our modern advances in technology have enabled us to encounter more extreme differences more regularly than ever before. We are navigating hyperdifference without the social technology or mental bandwidth to interpret or interact with it lovingly. Often, the natural psychological response to this overwhelm is withdrawal. We make our worlds small enough to be intelligible again, placing boundaries and limits on the people we can love and pay attention to. However, we worship a God who transcends all limits and denies separation. As Paul writes:

> For I am convinced that neither death, nor life, nor angels, nor rulers, nor things present, nor things to come, nor powers, nor height, nor depth, nor anything else in all creation, will be able to separate us from the love of God in Christ Jesus our Lord.
> (Romans 8:38–39)

God's great gift to us is an everlasting denial that the mental walls we erect through our lack of understanding have the power to cut us off from God and one another. Through Christ, God makes the unintelligible relatable. We are transformed not by *what* we know but by *who* we know. Christ is our partial window into viewing creation through God's eyes. Through Christ, we might come some way towards perceiving how God sees us, laying the foundation to love in whole what we can only know in part.

We might acknowledge that God's boundless love and unfailing strength dissolves all separation, but we might not trust interfaith engagement as a mechanism by which God seeks to build the kingdom. When I speak openly about my interfaith engagement activities with other Christians at church, in education settings or in the workplace, I have sometimes been met with confusion or – on rare occasions – suspicion. Implicit in the confusion is often the matter of prioritisation. I was once asked a question over dinner:

'Our congregations are dwindling, so why are you investing so much time and energy in reaching out to committed believers of other faiths rather than bringing the gospel to a secular society?' There might be a genuine anxiety for my and others' salvation at the root of the suspicion.[3] Good friends from my university Christian Union have taken me aside and asked directly, 'Are you taking on non-Christian beliefs and encouraging others to do the same?'

How did I respond to these questions? The beauty of the common life is its interdependence. The openness and hospitality we extend to people of other faiths has the capacity to surprise and draw in those who might be inclined to reject the Church as insular and hostile. We can all model a mutual flourishing that rejects polarisation and points to the source of all peace. This does not require a dilution of or deviation from doctrinal imperatives. We are not constructing a blended universal religion. Quite the opposite; we are on a mission from God. Interfaith engagement is an act of kingdom diplomacy to promote the common life through the gospel of peace.

Ambassadors for Christ donning the armour of God

I find it helpful to put some verses from Paul's letters side by side to expand on this bold claim:

> All this is from God, who reconciled us to himself through Christ, and has given us the ministry of reconciliation; that is, in Christ God was reconciling

the world to himself, not counting their trespasses against them, and entrusting the message of reconciliation to us. So we are ambassadors for Christ, since God is making his appeal through us; we entreat you on behalf of Christ, be reconciled to God.
(2 Corinthians 5:18–20)

Therefore take up the whole armour of God, so that you may be able to withstand on that evil day and having done everything, to stand firm. Stand therefore, and fasten the belt of truth around your waist, and put on the breastplate of righteousness. As shoes for your feet put on whatever will make you ready to proclaim the gospel of peace. With all of these, take the shield of faith, with which you will be able to quench all the flaming arrows of the evil one. Take the helmet of salvation, and the sword of the Spirit, which is the word of God.
(Ephesians 6:13–17 NRSV)

A dominant theme throughout Paul's letters is the offering of spiritual and practical guidance for living in conflict and tension within communities and as communities within communities. Paul's writings go some way towards signalling reconciliation and peace as a primary vocation for Christians. This is because reconciliation and peace sow the seeds for just relationships that draw us all more intimately into God's kingdom.

To answer this call and proclaim the message entrusted to us, we must take on the mantle of ambassadors of God's kingdom. At its simplest, the role of a diplomat is to act as a wise and effective conduit of communication to promote peaceful and prosperous relations; it is to interpret and relay messages that reflect the interests of the one who sent them. To do this successfully, diplomats must be fluent across languages and cultural specificities, so their messages are received and interpreted as intended.

To acquire such capability requires both confident clarity and creative flexibility. I'm drawn to Paul's armour of God metaphor in Ephesians 6 precisely because it expresses these qualities in tandem. Alongside the belt of truth that supports the breastplate of righteousness and the sword of the Spirit, we are told to put on 'whatever will make you ready to proclaim the gospel of peace' for shoes. Here, Paul seems to be acknowledging that peace is a pathway walked over uncertain and shifting terrain. There is no one-size-fits-all approach to peace; we must invest time in understanding the actions and steps appropriate for each context. Perhaps we need to borrow someone else's shoes, follow someone else's lead or adopt a new practice. Perhaps we need to work through serious discomfort as we wear shoes that need breaking in, going against our initial instincts and desires and trusting that the pain we are experiencing will get us somewhere. Ultimately, we need to discover and embed ways to promote God's diplomatic mission of 'reconciling the world to himself'.

What I have said so far could be read as a biblical case for culturally sensitive evangelism. What relevance does it have to interfaith engagement? Reconciliation is a living process between us and God, within ourselves and between us and others. In order to reconcile ourselves to one another across the multitude of our differences, we require an understanding that underpins peace as opposed to a fear that facilitates violence. That means accepting the existence of non-Christian worldviews as a social fact (perhaps even, controversially, a divine choice). According to the Pew Research Centre, Islam is the fastest growing world religion, and according to some projections, Muslims are due to be the largest faith group globally by 2070.[4] We must therefore make the active decision to engage constructively across these differences for our common life to flourish.

Reconciliation originates in God and flows through us to others, but this works in both directions. We are not entrusted by God simply to transmit God's message of reconciliation to others as we understand it but to receive it through and from others for our own sake. We do not only receive the message from fellow believers. Holiness that challenges and transforms our assumptions about what reconciliation is and who we are in God is found abundantly in those outside of our religious communities.[5]

I'm reminded here of the Imam of Muslim Welfare House in Finsbury Park, who in the minutes following the far-right terrorist attack on his mosque – when a van was deliberately driven into worshippers during Ramadan – put his body on the line to protect the perpetrator from reprisals until the police arrived and detained the suspect.[6] If that is not an example of peace and reconciliation as instinct, I'm not sure what is. God works through all

God's children and throughout creation towards mutual transformation.

I have found that the 'religious other' is a divine gift that deepens and facilitates our own redemption and that of all creation. This understanding should inspire and motivate us to engage across faiths confidently and creatively. The rest of this chapter will focus on the ways we might do this in our flexible peacemaking shoes.

Trusting through radical permission

'Don't you worry you're being a bit too fussy and difficult when you're a dinner guest?'

'Not even water! That's crazy!'

'Are you *really* choosing to cover?'

'If that statue is produced in a factory, what makes it holy?'

'What's the point of getting wet if it's a metaphor?'

'You don't cut your hair at all! Isn't that unhygienic?'

So many of our demarcations of faith are embodied: the clothes we wear, the food we eat and the rituals and festivals we participate in. These are the most notable and obvious signs of difference. They are imbued with meaning, but it is not necessarily simple to explain their significance to outsiders. Because they are so clearly personal, we are often afraid to have conversations about them at all for fear of causing offence.

Perhaps we recognise a time when we asked a question similar to those above and immediately cringed with embarrassment, seeing the visible discomfort it caused

– I know I have. What has been interesting to me as an interfaith practitioner is that such awkwardly worded questions need not shut down a conversation or provoke a hostile interaction; they can actually be the foundation for relationship building. The fact is that granting one another permission to have clumsy conversations in our everyday interactions is one of the most effective acts of generosity. So let's assume curiosity not cruelty, intrigue not incitement, and presume that others are open-hearted enough to afford us the same in return.

I remember facilitating a small interfaith discussion group where two of our Muslim students were asked every awkward question imaginable. The questions were rooted in common misconceptions and narratives about their faith. Normally, I would have intervened, but they were answering with such grace, confidence and enthusiasm that I felt that I had to let them continue. For them, this was an opportunity to practise *dawah*, the act of conveying the message of Islam to non-believers. They understood that the questions were not malicious and repaid them in kind with robust and humorous explanations that left everyone better informed and excited to explore more about their identities together in the future.

It is important at this juncture to acknowledge that sensitivity is still required. Historically, marginalised groups – who might often be the subject of our intercultural or religious curiosity – have been hurt by such explorations. While questions about faith identity can give us an insight into the complex person in front of us, we must remember that no one is there to be interrogated simply for our learning and categorisation of X or Y world view. Just imagine what it would feel like to be caught off guard at the receiving end of leading questions about your deep convictions when the other person is more interested in a 'gotcha moment' at your expense than in your answers.

But when done well, this kind of engagement can be one of the most powerful ways to build a relationship deeply and quickly – short-circuiting small talk and other awkward formalities – because we are getting to the heart of the things that matter, and seeing the passions, values and hopes of another person.

The example I always like to offer is a session run by the LSE Faith Centre on its interfaith leadership retreat.[7] Students who have only known one another for a few hours are put into three paired conversations of ten minutes' duration. Each person has five minutes to elaborate on an identity prompt, while the other can only ask probing questions. Then they swap places. This session runs in the evening. It is the last activity of the day, so students have free time from the moment the formal session is over. And yet, without fail, they stay. They stay and talk long into the early hours and then emerge bleary-eyed in the morning as deeply connected friends.

The questions I included at the beginning of this section are stylised snippets of genuine questions I have overheard students ask in these late-night discussions. When read in that context, they take on a whole new meaning (go back and look)! When we stop fearing the intentions of the other, we have a firm foundation for mutual discovery. Granting and receiving permission to have clumsy conversations is the first step we can take in our peacemaking shoes.

Treading on sacred ground

It was an uncomfortably hot July in 2018. Sitting in a small, stuffy room with a fraying carpet were ten young Christians and Muslims from the UK and the Middle East. In their hands were printouts of extracts from the Bible and the Qur'an that spoke to a particular theme: revelation. This could have been a heady topic to engage with in near sauna-like conditions, yet the atmosphere was electric. The conversation flowed from Jesus' divinity, to hadith science, to explanations and refutations of the Trinity, to understandings of ascension and paradise. Participants in the room found points of agreement and contention in unexpected places, leaving the conversation enriched and challenged.

This practice is called 'scriptural reasoning'. It is a particular method of interfaith engagement that puts holy texts at the centre of discussion. It emerged out of an academic adaptation of a rabbinic tradition of textual reasoning and has been used for decades as a dialogue tool to bring together religious believers – whether clerics, students or prisoners – so they can explore how they each understand reality through their faith.[8] My first introduction to scriptural reasoning was at a youth peacebuilding programme sponsored by the Archbishop of Canterbury and the Grand Imam of Al-Azhar and facilitated by the Rose Castle Foundation.[9] Every morning, we would break into small groups and discuss a different topic with relevant extracts of text. For me, these were some of the most precious and revealing moments on the programme.

As a Christian, I find that there is nothing more invigorating than reading the Bible through the fresh eyes of those who share few assumptions. Some of the most profound questions I have had to wrestle with in my Christian life have come from colleagues of other faiths, and I have been so grateful for their insights, challenges and queries over the years. They have strengthened my confidence in the gospel. Often, those who practise scriptural reasoning say that, ultimately, they engage in it for God's sake, as – for a moment – they share sacred ground with one another in the pursuit of truth.

Scriptural reasoning also has a deeply human, interpersonal element. When practised regularly, it is an illuminating window into the shared imagination that informs the everyday lives and choices of believers. It is also an encouraging place to observe respectful religious disagreement within traditions and to address any mistaken impression we might have that these are simple, monolithic worldviews. Over time, these insights evolve into instincts. You develop a deeper sensitivity that converts your encounters from clumsy to graceful, strengthening the potential for relationship. The trust that extends from an acknowledgement that there is a deep mutual understanding of something core to your being is hard to underplay.

Much has been written about scriptural reasoning, resulting in some fantastic guidance and resources on how to engage in it.[10] I hope that you may be sufficiently intrigued and inspired to give it a go yourself. Although it might feel a bit abstract, the sacred ground we come to share through dialogue not only enables the pursuit of truth(s) but becomes a solid foundation for joint action and mission within the common life.

Transforming through common interest

It was another blazingly hot July, this time in 2023. The streets of Cairo were afforded little shade or protection from the unrelenting sun. The air was still and the Nile, was in drought and at a concerningly low level, offering no relief. In an unassuming office, a cohort of young Islamic and Christian clerics and preachers were reflecting on the climate emergency.[11] They included young male and female scholars and preachers from Al-Azhar University, Coptic seminary students and nuns, as well as Anglican clerics and activists. The political climate and relationships between religious communities in Egypt had suffered greatly from the activities of Islamic State and other militant groups, who had carried out targeted atrocities across the country over the previous decade. So, while this gathering might not seem radical to those in plural societies, it was a remarkable testament to the patient and dedicated relationship building between senior religious leaders across these groups, who, during those moments of potential peril, had intermittently taken part in scriptural reasoning and other dialogue practices.

The intention of the gathering was to facilitate the production of a more locally produced, more intelligible discourse on climate change. The UN-sponsored scientific discourse many of us are used to in the West has little resonance in Egypt and the wider Middle East and is mistrusted as yet another form of foreign interference.[12] Our time together centred instead around religious texts, so the climate emergency might be framed as both a moral question and one rooted in the distinct religious traditions present.[13]

The shift from scepticism to animation that took place in front of my eyes was one of the most encouraging professional moments of my career. Witnessing a Muslim scholar reference a biblical passage and a Coptic seminarian reference a hadith to support their joint reflections on just stewardship was nothing less than the gospel of peace breathed into life. A new thirst for collaboration had eclipsed a preoccupation with segregation.

New collaborations of this nature are not only necessary in terms of reconciling our differences; they are urgent. Our approach to global challenges, of which the degradation of our shared home is the most pressing, are enhanced by the innovation and wisdom generated by our divergences in conversation. There is an untapped moral and spiritual solidarity waiting to be unleashed on the systemic injustices produced by our globalised secular power structures.

Hope in our hands

So perhaps, we should return to where we started – with a group of young Jews, Muslims and Christians standing at the altar of despair, the separation barrier in East

Jerusalem. Christian hope is not just the redemption of brokenness, it is redemption *through brokenness*. Christ's body was broken for us, and it is through that brokenness that we are redeemed. When he appeared to the apostles, Christ retained the holes in his hands and his pierced side. The scars that remain by painful repair are the perpetual testimony that wounds can heal.

That healing starts in our immediate environment, wherever we find ourselves. It might involve making the choice to reach out to our neighbour out of curiosity and not necessity; taking an active interest in their perspective; making radical leaps of trust; initiating conversations across difference – however clumsy; holding what is holy to us dear and inviting others to share sacred ground; seeing the infinite possibilities for justice when we build a solidarity of wisdom.

Every wound we heal in every place, in every time, serves to counter every other wound, old and new. We might not witness the healing of the biggest wounds in our lifetime. We might feel that we live in an age where wounds are opening up far faster than any are closing. But 'the light shines in the darkness, and the darkness did not overcome it' (John 1:5).

It is not naive to see our own agency in this; to trust in the unseen effects of our actions towards another; to believe that one day, through God's grace, we will inhabit a world where walls will become irrelevant. This is our story, this is our song, and it is one we can sing as loudly and confidently with people of other faiths as with our sisters and brothers in Christ.

Reflection questions

1 'God is found abundantly in those outside of our religious communities.' How do you respond to this statement? Is it something that surprises or challenges you? If so, how and why?
2 What do you think of scriptural reasoning and interfaith dialogue more generally? Is it something you would be interested to try? If yes, why? If not, what are your hesitations?
3 How might you and your church community become ambassadors for Christ wearing shoes for peacemaking? What does this mean in practice?

© Don Binder

Martha Jarvis is the Anglican Communion's Permanent Representative to the United Nations. She works with a small team to create bridges between the Church's work and the UN's – raising the Church's voice in international negotiations and creating partnerships between churches and UN teams responding locally to conflict, climate change and forced movement of people. She has also worked in the archbishop of Canterbury's reconciliation ministry, supporting church-led peacemaking in South Sudan and Mozambique, and managing the international growth of an initiative born of the ministry – the Difference course – which aims to mobilise a generation of peacemakers. This followed her early career in business development in Moldova, the Gulf and Southeast Asia. Throughout it all, she's seen nothing that compares to the power of reconciliation – of people coming back together after conflict, and ultimately of people coming back to God through Jesus.

Bible quotations in this chapter are taken from the NIV.

4

Wild paths of peace

We were in the sports stadium because the cathedral was too small. Thousands were moving to their seats before the service began. Zelfina – assistant to Mozambique's Presiding Bishop Carlos Matsinhe – stood in the central aisle fielding questions from left and right, lines of concentration appearing beneath her undercut bob. There was a buzz in the crowd gathered around her. The archbishop of Canterbury was preaching at the service and would momentarily appear in the procession. I watched, along with the archbishop's small staff team, feeling every emotion of those making the final preparations. Zelfina turned to handle the next demand and her navy and orange patterned dress flared out in her wake.

Behind her, a sea of people wearing the same material – styled uniquely in bomber jackets, waistcoats, wraps and fish-tail skirts – stretched across one-third of a stand, making up the choir. Close harmonies and deep rhythms moved the whole stadium. It was music that split the sinews of your heart. The remaining stands were packed with Mozambicans and some Angolans, young and old, who were there to celebrate the phenomenal growth and now independence of their church.

At this point, Mozambique was thirty years beyond the end of a civil war between the established government

(Frelimo) and an armed resistance movement (Renamo). The conflict is estimated to have killed nearly one million people. This day might have been about unity and celebration, but the legacy of that conflict was clearly present. Near the very end of the service, the retired Bishop Dinis Sengulane was called upon to offer his greetings. Bishop Dinis had been the most senior Mozambican in the Anglican Church for decades, including all sixteen years of the civil war. Along with other church representatives, he had led mediation efforts at the height of the violence that had enabled representatives of the two sides, Frelimo and Renamo, to talk. At great risk to his own life, he had crossed dividing lines, travelling into unknown, violently held territory to sit down with politicians and military leaders. Bishop Dinis had worked on a dialogue process for years until a peace agreement was signed. Following that, he established a gun amnesty which resulted in over one million guns being removed from civilian hands and turned into tools for farming, artworks and crosses.[1]

Only slightly stooped by age, Bishop Dinis walked across the stage with a cross made from recycled guns swinging gently across his front. As he looked up at the congregation, his eyes pinpricks of mischievous wisdom, the stadium erupted. Cheers rippled across the stands and along the floor, reaching a volume and continuing for a length of time I had rarely experienced in church. He raised a hand for quiet and spoke into the microphone, '*Ola, paz!*' (Hello, peace!) '*Ola, paz!*' resounded back at him from thousands of Mozambicans.

A battle ends

This is the hope that often motivates Christian peacemaking. It is a hope that conflict will stop, guns will become ploughshares, mourning will become celebration, and the Church will have a leading role in that transformation. In Mozambique, it was remarkable to behold.

The scale could seem very different, but we might know what this peace feels like in our own relationships. I remember a time when I approached someone I had wronged with an apology. I can still feel the sickening, churning sensation in my stomach as I waited while they looked me in the eye, acknowledged the impact my actions had had and then didn't hold the wrong against me. We turned a new page in our relationship, and it felt like Mozambique's choirs were singing in my soul. On other occasions, I have sat with friends, family and colleagues in uncomfortable conversations in which we have wrestled together with misunderstandings and difficulties in our relationships. With time and care, we descended through layers of superficial irritation to identify the underlying causes of tension. Once those causes were known, understood and released, the same conversations became the foundation of greater trust and intimacy. What had felt like swords pressing in upon sensitivities and resistance became the tools (or ploughshares) of our work and growth together.

The things that make for peace in our personal conflicts are closer to international examples than we might think. National peace like Mozambique's depends on an alignment of people turning from violence internationally, nationally and locally. Only God has ultimate control over that, and there are legal, financial and historic systems with significant influence, but individual choice is present at each level. The peace we make in our relationships matters, whether those choices affect our family, our workplace, our community or an entire nation.

Wherever we experience peace in our relationships, it is an echo of biblical shalom – a completeness that mirrors the completeness of God. This is not a shallow sense of peace that comes from avoiding difficult conversations, having our own way all the time or papering over the cracks of wrong and injustice. It is a deep peace that comes from expressing truth, living with justice and loving others generously. Holding those together creates the kind of wholeness we see in Psalm 85, often literally translated 'Love and faithfulness meet together, righteousness and peace kiss' (Psalm 85:10). In that meeting and that kiss, we see an image of the wholeness of the heavenly new creation in which humans and God live together in dynamic, life-giving relationships with each other and with creation (see Revelation 21–22).

But the war continues

Yet, so often, our hope that this peace can break into our lives is fragile and fleeting. For each of the moments of peace I have experienced, there are many others in which I have tried to be honest and it has only made things worse, or been involved in efforts aimed at healing that have become painful and divisive.

Likewise, in Mozambique, although the civil war has ended, the most recent round of local elections was fraught with tension between Frelimo and Renamo, and the Church's handling of events came under intense criticism. In the north east, a new insurgency has emerged, styled on Al Shabaab, which has claimed over 2,000 lives in the most brutal circumstances. Decades of resentment and desperation built up in this region as foreign investment did little to benefit local communities. Stark inequalities and unacknowledged injustice meant that unemployed youth were easy targets for recruitment into violent groups. Faith and traditional leaders, led by the Anglican Bishop Manuel Ernesto, are responding to draw communities together, enable dialogue, name injustice and provide essential trauma care, provision for refugees and engagement for youths, but the impact has been devastating.

As I write, violence also rips through the Middle East, Sudan, Ukraine, Myanmar, Nigeria, DRC, Papua New Guinea and many more places than I can list. It can leave us wondering what we are hoping for.

Reflection questions

1 Which aspect of wholeness is the hardest to find in our world, your culture or your close relationships: truth, justice or mercy?
2 Where do you feel the greatest unmet need for peace?

A different path is possible

Hope in these situations can sound trite – as if we are glossing over the injustices of today, telling people to suck up their anguish or to wait for peace in heaven. When a wilderness of conflict stretches before us, this kind of hope will keep us at the edge. We might watch things unfold and become overwhelmed by what we see, as is often the case when faced with coverage through the twenty-four-hour news cycle. Or we might stop caring about the damage caused by conflict that seems so normal. Alternatively, we might plunge into the wilderness and join in the battles. We quickly adopt the methods of our opponents, but at least it feels like we will bring justice through our own hands.

We need some strong motivation to take a different approach. In Mozambique, twelve years into the civil war, this was what the church faced. People died and were killed almost every day. The church leaders were desperate, and when they spoke to the government, they were told, 'But there is no other way. We have to continue fighting.' There must have been the temptation to join in or to accept the status quo, but the church chose something different. They ran a series of Bible studies to discover more about God's peace. What they saw there made them convinced that more must be possible beyond the civil war.

Believing was one thing; it was entirely another to *show* that a different way was possible. For that, the church leaders needed to identify people willing to talk to those whom they considered enemies. Representatives of the armed groups were hard to find. Some didn't want to talk, there was great danger in seeking them out and the continued devastation of the conflict risked any fragile confidence they established. Church leaders worked systematically over numerous trips around the region to engage with representatives and build trust that dialogue could be a legitimate alternative to violence. After years of painstaking conversations like this, a peace agreement was finally signed.

Hope does not guarantee a particular outcome, nor does it somehow enable us to endure, unfeeling, until Jesus returns. Instead, hope in a future secure with God gives us a different perspective on the present. Through it, we can reimagine the wilderness of conflict from God's point of view. Stretching across the barren landscape, we see the wild paths of peace. When the church in Mozambique showed that it was possible to walk those paths, others followed.

We can do the same in our lives. In Revelation, we read that in the new heaven and new earth, God will wipe the tears from our eyes, pain and death will end and the leaves of the tree of life will be for the healing of the nations (see Revelation 21–22). When we believe that, however fragile and far off it might seem in our immediate circumstances, it can change the paths we follow now. When we believe that God sees us and will wipe away our tears (Revelation 21:4), we might stop needing to have the last word in every disagreement. When we believe that God will bring all nations together in the heavenly city (Revelation 7:9), we might seek out stronger relationships now with people who represent those nations. When we know that God's plan is for humans and nature to live in beautiful balance (Revelation 22:2), we might rethink the ways we currently treat the earth.

Reflection question

Where does the difference between the new earth and your current relationships seem most stark? How could you pray for change in that area?

Hope needs faith and love

Although hope gives us the eyes to see the paths, we need other guides to keep us going. If hope is the perspective of the future, faith can offer us the perspective of the past. In the wilderness, faith allows us to stand our ground as fog or darkness descend. When we can barely understand what is happening in a conflict, we need to draw on what we have previously known of God's goodness. We step out, with our questions and laments, believing that God's goodness remains and that following him is what we need to do.

In the wilderness, ultimately love is what renders any journey along these paths bearable, bringing colour to what is otherwise beige, connection where there was only division, and making it seem worthwhile to carry on.

The three perspectives of hope, faith and love can be seen working together when Jesus encounters Martha and Mary shortly after their brother Lazarus has died. Martha's

Wild paths of peace

faith drives her to act and believe. She goes out to meet Jesus, believing that the goodness and power she has seen in him remains true. She is also indignant, because of that belief, that he has turned up after Lazarus could have been healed (see John 11:21–22). In response, Jesus leads her into hope not only in the ultimate resurrection but in the power of his resurrection life now.

When Jesus meets with Mary, she is in floods of tears. He doesn't tell her to pull herself together because of a future hope in ultimate resurrection or in the miracle he is about to perform in raising her brother to life. He is so deeply engaged in that moment, so tightly connected to her sorrow and to the loss of his own friend Lazarus, that he simply weeps with her (see John 11:35).

What Jesus does next, in bringing life where there was only loss, produces an outpouring of contagious hope. Many others begin to follow him. But it also produces disbelief, tension and opposition (see John 11:45–53). The paths of God's peace are wild – full of risk, challenge and sometimes resistance. It is only a powerful combination of hope, faith and love that will motivate us to find those paths and keep going along them.

Keeping faith amid division

'Your faith should not stand in the wisdom of men, but in the power of God,' said Uncle Ray Minniecon, quoting 1 Corinthians 2:5. There was a steely conviction beneath his soft tones, steel forged in generations of faithfulness through injustice. Uncle Ray is an Aboriginal Christian pastor living in what is now known as Sydney, Australia.[2] He dates his walk with Jesus back to the 1870s, when a missionary was reading the Bible with a group of enslaved people on a sugar cane farm. That night, the missionary wrote in her diary that the Holy Spirit fell on those present. One of those assembled was Uncle Ray's grandfather. Generations later, Uncle Ray himself experienced the same Spirit-filled conviction.

I met him, with others working for the Archbishop of Canterbury's Reconciliation Ministry, over grainy video calls during the Covid-19 lockdowns. As night fell in the Australian winter, Uncle Ray would appear in a beanie hat with a scarf wrapped around his neck, showing the black, red and yellow of the Aboriginal flag, which represented the colours of his people, land and sun. These calls made a deep impact. We moved between moments of intense silence, floored by the profundity of what had just been shared, to moments of released laughter and unexpected joy.

Over the time period in which Uncle Ray traced the spread of Christianity through his ancestors, many indigenous peoples, including his family, suffered greatly at the hands of the Church. Between 1910 and 1970, over 100,000 Aboriginal and Torres Strait Islander children were separated from their parents under the Child Removal Policy. Under this policy, children of indigenous parents could be forcibly removed from their families and placed in state or church-run orphanages and homes. Many children were beaten, forced not to speak their native language or practise their family's traditions. Some were raped or killed, and in many places, church organisations and professing Christians were complicit. The ramifications of this policy continue to this day. Australia's indigenous peoples are 12.5 times as likely to be incarcerated as non-indigenous peoples and 2.5 times as likely to take their own lives.

Uncle Ray wrestled with this history for years and worked directly with those suffering mentally and physically with its consequences. Incredibly, his faith not only survived but determined the course of his actions and character throughout. When we met him, he was creating bridges between the institutions he held accountable for this suffering – the Anglican Church among them – and the survivors of that suffering. He had set up an Aboriginal church within an Anglican church in Sydney, which he hoped would encourage relationships of understanding and healing to develop.

The primary reason for doing so was because of his faith in the nature of God. He said once that his people didn't experience grace and love from the government or from the Church, but they did experience it from 'knowing who the Spirit of the Lord was among us.' That past experience of God, from the Holy Spirit falling on his ancestors to his own encounters with God's living presence, was enough to shape the trajectory of his life and the way he lived each moment.

For many indigenous Christians, this still has great costs. They continue to face criticism, misunderstanding and arrogance when they voice what they have experienced and what needs to change to address underlying imbalances of power and perception. They sacrifice time, energy, reputation and more to engage in dialogue that might amount to nothing or might be used against them. Some of these sacrifices, and the historic injustices their people have suffered, can never be repaid.

Yet through their faith emerges hope. Uncle Ray and others have sought out stronger relationships with the Church, showing that grace and generosity are possible even as great injustices are named and where institutions have failed. That can give hope in our own lives that we need not shy away from naming what is wrong, or feel crushed when others point that out in us and the cultures we represent. It can also encourage us to look beneath the surface of the institutions and communities of which we are part, to question who might have been excluded or damaged by our accepted practices. Where changes are needed, it can give us the courage to repent, pray and act, even if we don't yet see where that path will lead. God is at work to restore. We can have faith in that.

Reflection question

I love the language that Psalm 34 uses: 'Taste and see that the LORD is good' (Psalm 34:8). With faith, we can call to mind God's goodness like we call to mind our favourite meal – something that was a lived reality known in the body and heart.

Where have you tasted the goodness of God in the past, especially in times of conflict or division? How could you offer something of that goodness to others, even if it is not returned?

Deepening love amid violence

In 2019, the leaders of the three largest churches in South Sudan – Anglicans, Catholics and Presbyterians – invited South Sudan's politicians to a retreat at the Vatican. It was the fulfilment of an idea suggested by Madam Rebecca Garang, an influential South Sudanese political leader searching for ways to bring her country together. At that point, the politicians had been unable to form a government after six years of intense conflict. One of them was still banished from the country. Yet they came together in that retreat and sat in a room alone for the first time since a shoot-out in the capital, Juba, that had killed 300 people in only a few days.

At the very end, Pope Francis got up from delivering his formal address, following an impulse that was not in the script for the retreat. The room held its breath. He implored the politicians simply: 'As a brother, remain in peace ... I ask you from the heart, let us move forward.' He then approached them and, from his not insignificant height, knelt down on the floor and kissed each politician's feet. It was a moment when time seemed to shape itself around the movement of the Holy Spirit. We were not watching the normal progression of seconds and minutes but the radiation of God's love and light into a single act.

These moments of depth in the present do not stop conflict, nor do they ignore its impact, but they somehow hold at bay the forces of negativity, death and destruction so we feel human again: known, held and alive. In this kind of love, we find remarkable experiences of healing and wholeness in connection with others that are the very heartbeat of peacemaking. They are moments that bring hope because they can change who we are and therefore how we act amid division.

Love like this has transformative power because it reflects God's own move towards us. We can easily miss this if we have a purely moral sense of sin. We can assume that God accepts us passive aggressively while secretly holding what we have done and what we will do against us. Instead, Paul describes God's move towards us in peacemaking terms: 'God was reconciling the world to himself in Christ, not counting people's sins against them' (2 Corinthians 5:19). When we trust in Jesus, God sees in us something restored to what it was meant to be. The relationship that was once divided is now whole. Each moment of each day, God extends to us the possibility of knowing a relationship upheld with justice, truth and mercy. The peace we know from that is incomparable.

Reflection question

How do you speak about this restored relationship with God in your prayers? How is it reflected in church services that you attend?

Peace with God might be incomparable, but we can extend the love it is founded on to others. Sometimes, we extend this love in solidarity with those travelling seemingly impossible paths of peace. Mama Harriet Baka, the Provincial Coordinator of the Mothers' Union in South

Sudan, is small only in stature. In force of nature, in faith, in conviction and in truth telling, she is towering. Following the 2016 shoot-out in Juba, Mama Harriet and others ventured out of the city to the newly created Protection of Civilians Camp with basic supplies for the women who were too scared to leave the compound to find firewood and simple food. In the years that followed, Mama Harriet and the rest of the Mothers' Union continued to work across tribal lines in that same camp to enable the women there to set up literacy programmes and savings groups. These were lifelines in a situation that remained tragically stagnant, as those sheltering waited for a stable peace agreement to allow them to return home safely. Here, love took on a practical, hope-enabling form.

Reflection question

Who needs your love in solidarity with their experience of conflict or division? Where do you need to receive this kind of love?

Sometimes, we offer this love to challenge an unloving status quo. In 2023, the sun was setting over a crowd of around 70,000 of every tribe and denomination in Juba. Some of the crowd had walked for days to be there. Archbishop Justin Welby was preaching at an ecumenical service as part of a Pilgrimage of Peace he was taking with the Pope and the Moderator of the (Presbyterian) Church of Scotland to follow up the retreat at the Vatican. A transitional government had formed from the politicians whose feet the Pope had kissed, but it was fragile, with the implementation of the peace agreement well off-track and community-level violence escalating. It was rare for the people of South Sudan to gather in such numbers with such unity. Just behind Archbishop Justin sat Pope Francis, looking out at people he had spoken about and prayed for regularly for over a decade. On the other side, the Moderator, Dr Iain Greenshields, was readying himself to deliver the next part of the service. I stood at the very back of the stage, watching the light fade, hearing the chatter of the security guards from the rear gates and feeling the intensity of that moment like you feel the humidity before a storm.

Suddenly, a cry rose up from the women in the crowd – yodelling and cheering that filled the night air. Archbishop Justin had just called for an end to sexual and domestic violence, in effect the suffering that would have been experienced by the vast majority of women there. He had seen them and voiced their pain. These were women who had an incredible capacity for love amid violence. I had sat with a number of them and would count a handful now as friends. I had seen some of them cry and scream in prayer. I had seen others with faces hardened to masks, as if their bodies were creating impenetrable cases over their hearts and souls, which bore the scars of trauma. And yet they had embraced me like a sister or daughter, cared about my cares and hoped for my hopes. They had engaged me in such a depth of life and laughter that it was impossible not to give the present my full attention. Archbishop Justin's words might not have changed anything immediately, but rejoicing, like a thunderclap of love and understanding, echoed from leader to people and between brother and sisters.

That moment didn't fix the conflict, but the church leaders had shown their commitment to accountability for every form of violence and challenged an unloving status quo. The commitments made at the Vatican had not been forgotten. Worsening conditions were named, and the voice of the people was heard.

Reflection question

Does your love come with accountability? And does your accountability come with love?

Sometimes, we offer this love to enemies. Jesus' command to 'love your enemies and pray for those who persecute you' (Matthew 5:44) makes that clear.

This command can be taken too lightly and used to suggest that the love of enemies means that we ignore the wrongs done to us. That can be particularly damaging in situations of abuse, where it could lead to silence, repeat offence and toxic proximity. Instead, more powerfully, the love of enemies upholds the need for truth and justice, affirming the dignity owed to us as children of God and yet also maintaining a defiant posture of the heart that says that even our enemies were made by God, even they have dignity and even they can be transformed by him. Offering that kind of love is costly, because often those on 'our side' do not understand.

Bishop Anthony Poggo, Secretary General of the Anglican Communion, was bishop in a diocese in South Sudan that was attacked by a neighbouring tribe in 2014. The son of one of their lay readers was killed, and there was nothing the clergy could do to stop a group of their own youth taking up arms in revenge. Instead, many of the churchgoers set about providing medical care and shelter for those of the opposing tribe, making themselves unpopular by caring for their enemies. However, their actions led church leaders in the opposing tribe to take note and to speak with their own youth before things escalated further. They were open to a meeting with Bishop Anthony, which eventually led to peace talks and a quietening of violence.

In moments like this, we are taking the costly, life-giving path that God has taken with us and offering love where others are not acting from or experiencing true wholeness in relationship. We are using what conflict cannot take from us, and these are the things that have the power to transform.

> And now these three remain: faith, hope and love. But the greatest of these is love.
> (1 Corinthians 13:13)

Reflection question

This defiant posture of the heart towards enemies has the power to break cycles of revenge, reaction and learned behaviour. Where do you want that power to be at work? How could that shape your prayers?

Wild paths that inspire hope

Meeting and working with the people mentioned above has shown me that different ways are possible amid individual and systemic conflict. The hope that this has inspired is powerful. It does not depend on a guaranteed outcome; it depends on individuals making the choice, however imperfectly, to walk into the wilderness of conflict and pursue the wild paths of peace as Jesus would have done. Where they tread, others can follow.

These untamed paths are not easy. They involve risk and sometimes sacrifice. Often, they are unpopular paths to take. But they contain riches of God's grace that are unavailable if we stay at the edge of the wilderness, accepting the status quo, waiting for heaven to arrive or joining in with the battles.

John Paul Lederach, a well-known Mennonite mediator and peacemaker, puts it like this: 'Deep conflicts are stressful and painful. At worst, they are violent and destructive. Yet at the same time, they create some of the most intense spiritual encounters we experience. Conflict opens a path, a holy path, towards revelation and reconciliation.'[3]

If we do not follow these paths and show that a different way is possible, who will?

Cathrine Fungai Ngangira was born and raised in Zimbabwe. She served in youth ministry in the Diocese of Harare and the Anglican Church in Zimbabwe and is now Priest-in-Charge of Boughton-under-Blean with Dunkirk, Graveney with Goodnestone and Hernhill in the Diocese of Canterbury. Cathrine contributed to the journal *Modern Believing* in 2021 on the topic 'The Value of Ubuntu as a Framework for Leadership in Christian Ministry'.

Alongside parish ministry, she is a member of the advisory group of USPG's Fellowship of Anglican Scholars of Theology and a member of the Council of St John's College, Durham.

Bible quotations in this chapter are taken from the NRSVUEA.

5

Hope and the Church of England

The Shona proverb *muzivi wenzira yeparuvare ndiye mufambi wayo*, translated, 'The one who knows the way on the rocks is the one who walks it,' speaks to the wisdom of those who have travelled through difficulties – people who have gained an insight into the complexities of the path ahead and how they can be navigated. I will be reflecting on this and drawing on my personal experience as I offer some thoughts on the current state of life and ministry in the Church of England.

Coming from Zimbabwe, I grew up with the impression that the Church of England was dying, and that big old church buildings were pretty much all that was left. So, when I arrived in England in 2016, you can imagine how surprised I was to discover that some church communities were thriving. I have since experienced vibrant worship in London churches, flourishing Durham–Newcastle churches and day-to-day life in the rural parishes of Kent, where I now serve. Admittedly, church attendance continues to decline, and the cultural relevance of Christianity is questioned, but even in uncertainty, I dare to hope.

What is going on?

One beautiful summer afternoon, I was out walking in the Hernhill and Dunkirk countryside, which is dotted with fields and patches of woodland. Sometimes, as you follow a path, you will come across the remnant of a war memorial – a subtle reminder of this area's poignant history now reclaimed by nature. On this occasion, I was accompanied by a young lady named Tariro (a Shona name meaning 'hope'). Tariro's interest in exploring the Christian faith had been ignited by her philosophy studies and the way of being she had observed in her Christian classmates.

As we walked along the quiet country lanes, we discussed the fundamentals of the Christian faith, and I tried to explain to her the various theological views, practices and beliefs of those who make up the Church of England. Then she asked a question that was both exciting and scary and stopped me in my tracks.

'Where do you see the Church of England in thirty years' time?'

As I paused to think, I noticed that our path had just been intersected by another. That seemed particularly poignant, for at this moment, ministry and life in the Church of England feels a lot like life at the crossroads.

Being at a crossroads is a powerful and provocative image. We often connect it with a critical point in decision-making. You might like to reflect for a moment on a time when you have been at a crossroads physically or metaphorically. How did it feel?

Whenever I think of a crossroads, I think of the cross of Christ. As a symbol of Christianity, the cross reminds us of the passion and death of Jesus Christ: there at the cross, where good and evil converged, he was crucified for our salvation. This biblical image reminds me that being at a crossroads demands discernment and decision-making. For example, think of the two thieves crucified with Jesus and the choices each of them made about his identity.

The crossroads of the cross is a place where God's people are called to choose between life and death, faithfulness and rebellion. It also represents the tension between suffering and transformation, hurt and healing, hopelessness and hope. It represents not only the opportunity to change the direction of travel but the possibility of significant spiritual transformation.

In his article, 'The Church of England after COVID: quo vadis?', David Goodhew predicts that, if current trends continue, the church might become a 'tiny remnant' or vanish entirely in many places within twenty years.[1]

Quo vadis? – 'Where are you going?' – is, according to Christian tradition, the question that Peter asked on encountering the risen Christ along the Appian Way. Peter had fled persecution in Rome, but Christ's response – that he was going to be crucified again – led Peter to return to Rome to be crucified himself.

The Church of England faces a similar question: *Quo tendimus?* – 'Where are we going?'

The crossroads of diversity and inclusion

One of the most significant matters facing the Church of England is that of diversity and inclusion. Over the past decade, the church has made important strides in addressing issues relating to gender, race,[2] sexuality and safety.[3] The increasing number of women bishops and greater diversity in terms of leadership are definite signs of progress. However, reports of exclusion, racism and safeguarding failures suggest that the journey towards inclusion is far from complete. As a minister, I find myself at a crossroads: what if the time comes when I must choose between tradition and the need for radical change? What if the denomination that nurtured my faith divides over these issues? There is still so much work to be done.

As an ordained minister of Zimbabwean heritage, I have experienced both the joy and the challenges of serving in predominantly white communities. Many of my colleagues and parishioners have welcomed me so warmly that I have a deep sense of belonging within the Church of England. I have also experienced moments of exclusion and misunderstanding. In some communities, my cultural background and perspectives have not been fully valued or appreciated, and this has been painful to experience. Yet what gives me hope for the Church of England is that it still has people who are courageous enough to stand up for 'the truth'.

What is the truth in this context? In Galatians, Paul declares:

> There is no longer Jew or Greek; there is no longer slave or free; there is no longer male and female, for all of you are one in Christ Jesus. And if you belong to Christ, then you are Abraham's offspring, heirs according to the promise.
> (Galatians 3:28–29)

At its core, the Christian message calls for the radical inclusion of people of different cultures and backgrounds within the love of God. That is surely what should guide the church as it navigates this crossroads.

The crossroads of mission and ministry

There's an exhilarating description on the website of the Church of England:

> The Church of England seeks to be a Christian presence in every community, up and down the land. Each parish or group of parishes has a parish priest – a minister ordained (or set apart) for ministry, who leads the people in worship, teaches the faith and gives pastoral support to the people of the parish. And much of the ministry of the church is undertaken by lay people: the faithful Christian disciples who live out their faith in Jesus Christ in worship and service.[4]

But as exciting as this idea is, it's a challenge to interpret what 'presence' truly means. Parishes are increasingly amalgamating. One minister (or a small team of ministers) can be responsible for multiple parishes, leading to an increased amount of parish administration. Maintaining a visible presence in such conditions can sometimes seem like an impossible task, so it's vital to gain an understanding of what presence can mean and look like.

When I was licensed to serve five rural villages, I quickly realised that there was going to be a tension between being present with people and being overwhelmed by meetings, emails and administrative tasks. I decided to take inspiration from the ministry models I had observed in Zimbabwe. There, whenever a new vicar arrives in a parish, pastoral visits are a priority. I encouraged congregation members to invite their neighbours round when I visited or, alternatively, to introduce me to them.

I have also practised being present by attending school events and participating in local activities. This has opened up opportunities to talk about faith, God and spirituality that I might not otherwise have had, and I have seen people, young and old, responding to the message of Christ in small, meaningful ways. These have been signs of hope.

Presence, then, is often physical proximity, though that includes being attuned to the spiritual needs of the community. It means walking alongside people in the everyday challenges of their lives. It means joining with them in advocating for justice and environmental stewardship. It means taking every chance to plant seeds that might blossom into spiritual habits and familiarising people with the language of faith.

Finding hope at the crossroads

Of course, we might still be tempted to feel hopeless. Josef Pieper, in his book *On Hope*, identifies two forms of hopelessness: despair and presumption.[5] Despair is marked by a sense of pessimism that makes us think that our circumstances are beyond improvement, whereas presumption dismisses the need for engaging with God's grace. However, I believe that there is much to be learned by sitting with this tension.

Jürgen Moltmann, in his work *Theology of Hope*, suggests that, 'The contradictions to the existing reality of himself and his world in which man is placed by hope is the very contradiction out of which this hope itself is born – it is the contradiction between the resurrection and the cross.'[6]

For Moltmann, hope is an active force that drives us towards the future not yet realised but promised by God. Hope is not an escape from reality but a response to it. Hope is born from the very struggles and contradictions that characterise human existence, including the Christian life.

To be a Christian means being a prisoner of hope. In his post-exilic prophecy, the prophet Zechariah encourages his audience, 'Return to your stronghold, O prisoners of hope' (Zechariah 9:12). The call to return to the stronghold, which can be interpreted as the security of God's presence, is accompanied by a promise of double restoration. God will not only restore what was lost but will also bless the Israelites abundantly beyond their previous state.

The temptation for us today is to get excited about the promise and to miss the first part: that the return to God is preceded by a departure. This might be a physical or spiritual departure. It might be subtle or obvious. It might be justified or unjustified. The crucial thing is that being a prisoner of hope means that we are deeply bound to the belief that God is present, even when we find ourselves in painful or discouraging circumstances.

Hope: an image in contradiction

The image of a prisoner of hope makes me think of the painting *Hope* by George Frederick Watts. Here, Hope is depicted as a blindfolded woman, hunched and seated on a globe. Her head is bent as she listens to music playing on a lyre, all its strings broken except for one. The mood is dark and cold. G. K. Chesterton once commented that, at first glance, the title for the painting would seem to be *Despair*.

For many, sitting on the globe might symbolise elevation, empowerment and great accomplishment. Here, it represents the woman's confinement. Yet, though it's an uncomfortable place, she remains steadfast, grasping her single-stringed lyre firmly. It seems to me that the blindfolded woman in the painting illustrates the essence of hope; that she is imprisoned by hope.

Christian hope is directed towards the unseen. In Romans, we read:

> For in hope we were saved. Now hope that is seen is not hope, for who hopes for what one already sees?

> But if we hope for what we do not see, we wait for it with patience.
> (Romans 8:24–25)

Hope often thrives in uncertainty. It requires faith rather than mere optimism. It acknowledges our lack of complete understanding but assures us that even the limited knowledge we have can sustain our hope and trust in God.

The Diocese of Harare, where I began my ministry, once went through a period of political instability, economic collapse and social upheaval. Yet it remained a beacon of hope for many. The hymn 'Christian Seek Not Yet Repose' provided an anchor for people in the unknown.

Returning to the moody, subdued colours of the painting, we notice that directly above the woman's right shoulder there is a tiny star flickering faintly – a symbol of light in darkness. Hope clings to God's promises. As Hebrews 6:19 reminds us, 'We have this hope, a sure and steadfast anchor of the soul.' Hope is a confident expectation of God fulfilling his promises. The preceding verses emphasise that God's promises are unchanging and guaranteed by an oath. Those who persevere will receive the promise, as hope concerns both the present and the future realisation of God's purpose in creation.

A call to a wild bright hope

If the Church of England were to die in twenty years, as some predict, I believe that God would still be at work rebuilding his Church in new and unexpected ways.

We are at a crossroads, but it is not a place to remain. The challenge for the Church of England is to embrace the tension of this moment, to pause and reflect, and then to move forward with wild, bright hope – not a naive optimism but a deeply rooted trust that God is faithful and his Spirit is still leading us, beyond the cross, towards the empty tomb and the promise of new life.

Reflection questions

1 Where are the crossroads in your own faith journey or ministry?
2 How can you cultivate hope in the face of uncertainty?
3 What steps can you take to be more present in your community?

Keziah Patterson is the Archbishop of Canterbury's Parliamentary and Public Affairs Advisor and Researcher. She has been working for the archbishop in this area since September 2019, and her role involves supporting him in both his work as a lord spiritual – one of twenty-six bishops of the Church of England who sit in the House of Lords and take part in the business of the upper chamber of Parliament – and in his wider engagement in the public sphere on questions of policy and public affairs.

Keziah previously spent five years studying politics. She has been a Christian for as long as she can remember.

Bible quotations in this chapter are taken from the NIVUK.

6

A vision for hope in politics

I'm sitting in St Stephen's Hall, the large and grand chamber leading up to Central Lobby in the heart of Parliament. I'm here on my lunch break to pray and reflect, and despite being a main thoroughfare for Members of Parliament, peers and visitors, it's unusually silent. I spend around twenty-five minutes almost entirely alone, the hall still and empty apart from the rows of statues of famous parliamentarians from centuries past that line each side. Sunlight streams through the stained-glass windows, and I feel the presence of God very strongly in the beauty and quiet.

As the archbishop's parliamentary advisor, I've spent many days walking through Parliament, and the building itself constantly prompts me to gaze upwards. You might not realise it, but the Christian faith permeates the foundations of our political system, the walls and even the floors of Parliament, speaking of God's presence. Sitting in St Stephen's Hall, you cannot help but be reminded of God's faithfulness to us over the years.

A building full of God's presence

At the centre of the stone floor of Central Lobby, there is an inscription in Latin from the Psalms: 'Unless the LORD builds the house, the builders labour in vain' (Psalm 127:1).

A vision for hope in politics

The Moses Room in the House of Lords is where committee sessions are generally held. There, a large painting hangs on the wall. It shows Moses bringing the second set of stone tablets down from Mount Sinai: the law of God for his people.

Magnificent flying angels are carved into the beams supporting the ceiling of Westminster Hall, the oldest part of the Palace of Westminster, which was saved from the Great Fire of 1834 when much of the rest of the building was destroyed.

St Stephen's Hall itself stands on the site of what was originally the royal Chapel of St Stephen, a place of worship for kings and queens, before it became the debating chamber of the House of Commons (also sadly lost in the Great Fire). Powerful speeches would have been made here and brave stands taken by many heroes of history, including faithful Christians who worked in Parliament and the government in the service of our nation.

In my half-hour of contemplation, I feel surrounded and strangely reassured by these historical figures, as if God is reminding me that Christians today, in politics and Parliament, follow in the footsteps of many redoubtable souls.

I think of William Wilberforce and his famous words: 'God Almighty has set before me two great objects, the suppression of the slave trade and the reformation of manners.'[1] As a child, watching a film about his life and work was instrumental in my early sense of calling to enter the field of politics and government.

And then there's Lord Shaftesbury. A Member of Parliament from 1826, he was referred to by many as 'The Poor Man's Earl' because of his commitment to improving the lives of working people. He was instrumental in passing legislation in a number of areas, such as the care and treatment of the mentally ill and labour standards and regulations, including those affecting women and young people. He also championed free education for children from poor families. The impact Lord Shaftesbury had on people's everyday lives speaks eloquently to me of devotedness to God and of faith enacted in daily life.

Wilberforce and Shaftesbury are only two of the many who remind us, first, that the serious challenges and deep injustices we face today are not unique to our times and, second, that historically we have seen enormous strides towards a better society. I have great hope that God is still calling Christians to serve him, just as he has in the past. This really matters. We desperately need people of character and vision to stand up in politics today.

Hope for politics?

Over the past decade or so, a series of scandals has led some people to doubt politicians' commitment to the common good. Trust – that indispensable quality for the functioning and flourishing of societies – is hard won and very easily lost. We have seen declining levels of confidence in all who work in the government, along with rising verbal abuse and physical threats towards MPs and other public leaders, including the horrifying murders of MPs Jo Cox in 2016 and Sir David Amess in 2021.

I've felt very sad as I've witnessed the sharp increase in the kind of populist politics that divides people with deliberate nastiness, 'othering', lying and politicisation of serious issues for short-term political gain. Sometimes, the language used to refer to people – be they political opponents or individuals affected by various policies – has failed to recognise their dignity as human beings created in the image of God.

When we descend to the gutter, our ability to respond to the inevitable succession of crises is detrimentally impacted. It can feel like we have little resilience. Yet, despite all of this, I remain profoundly hopeful about what God might intend to do in our time.

Grounds for hope

What are the grounds for this hope?

In addition to the examples shown by heroes of history and the permeating of Parliament with Christian words and images that remind us that the Lord has been and always will be sovereign over everything, we have the promises of God in Scripture. In Isaiah's prophecy about Jesus, he says that, 'The government will be on his shoulders,' and that, 'Of the greatness of his government and peace there will be no end' (Isaiah 9:6–7). I love that this truth runs throughout the Bible – from God's great act of creation in Genesis to the final days when his everlasting kingdom will be established. It's almost as if God knew how often we would need to be reminded.

A vision for hope in politics

I've certainly seen rays of light in my time in politics, and I've been heartened by people who are noticeably working to be God's hands and feet in bringing about transformation. Politicians might be much maligned, but many of them are extraordinary public servants doing a difficult job that carries huge expectations, while having much more limited power than you might imagine. They often face social media storms and attacks from opposing colleagues, all while trying to bring some kind of work-life balance to what can be a brutally demanding schedule. And though some fail to live up to the expectations we put on them, others quietly serve their communities, often receiving very little credit for the personal cost this can exact.

There remains a strong Christian presence within Parliament, though I have to admit that this came as something of a surprise to me when I began to work for the archbishop.

For example, are you aware that a key task for the lords spiritual – the twenty-six bishops and archbishops who sit in the House of Lords – is to read prayers at the beginning of every day of business? Or that prayers are still said at the start of every sitting of the House of Commons? The Speaker of the House of Commons has a chaplain who is available to provide pastoral support to MPs, and lords spiritual fulfil this role for peers in the House of Lords. Services still take place regularly in the Chapel of St Mary Undercroft, built by King Edward I in 1297 (and subsequently further developed).

And there are many MPs and peers who are Christians, a number of whom I've had the privilege of meeting while working with the archbishop. I've often been struck by their humility and quiet dedication to particular issues and causes, and their openness about how their Christian faith strengthens and inspires them. For example, the Labour MP Sir Stephen Timms has served his community in East Ham faithfully for decades. Similarly, the former Conservative MP Sir Gary Streeter retired after more than thirty years as a local MP where I grew up in Devon. Both have taken a courageous and distinctive stand on many issues. You might not hear these good news stories in our media cycle, but that doesn't mean that they don't exist.

National Prayer Breakfast

One event which particularly impacted me was the 2022 National Parliamentary Prayer Breakfast in Westminster Hall in Parliament. These Prayer Breakfasts are held annually, and church leaders are encouraged to invite their local MPs to attend. The theme on this occasion was 'Serving the Common Good', and the Prime Minister and Leader of the Opposition – along with many ministers, MPs, peers and church leaders – heard a sermon by Revd Les Isaac, the founder of Street Pastors. He focused on Philippians 2:5–11, speaking about Jesus being a servant leader who humbled himself and encouraged us to serve others humbly and with integrity. After the sermon, I could sense God's presence powerfully in the room, and I was moved to tears as we sang the song 'We Seek Your Kingdom'. Set to the tune of the hymn 'Abide with Me', the final verse reads:

A vision for hope in politics

> Faithful to govern ever may we be
> Selfless in service, loving constantly
> In everything may your authority
> Transform, revive, and heal society.[2]

In the days following the breakfast, Sajid Javid, the Secretary of State for Health and Social Care, announced that he had lost confidence in Prime Minister Boris Johnson and was going to resign. He told the BBC that listening to Les Isaac's sermon on integrity was what had finally made up his mind,[3] and he began his resignation speech in Parliament by referencing the prayer breakfast.[4] Mr Javid's resignation was swiftly followed by a whole series of ministerial resignations, which led within days to the resignation of the Prime Minister himself.

Divine wisdom and solutions

I believe that there are two key ways in which Christians can respond to God's invitation to partner with him in the political sphere in order to bring transformation, revival and healing in society (as spoken of in our song).

The first is by being people who bring solutions. As Christians, we have the unique advantage of having access to the God of all wisdom (see James 1:5). Why would he not want us to speak to him about the challenges and difficulties we're facing? Why would he not want to offer his help?

When I was a student, I remember a group of us discussing a big policy question facing the UK at the time. Even our tutor, an expert in that area, was at a loss as to how to advise those in the government. I remember sensing the Holy Spirit whispering to me over and over in that moment, '*I have a solution, I have a solution, I have a solution,*' and inviting me to dream with him about solutions based on the principles of the kingdom of God.

I believe that as we pray and seek God, we can be given blueprints – divine downloads from heaven – on how to address the problems we're facing, whether big or small. God cares about our work and our daily lives, whatever sector we're involved in, and I believe that he has things to say to us about these if we simply ask him.

Political reconciliation

The second way we can partner with God in political life is to fulfil our role as peacemakers (see Matthew 5:9) as we promote and seek political reconciliation. We're never going to get to a place where everyone in politics agrees with one another (that would be unanimity, not reconciliation), but as Archbishop Justin Welby says, it's possible for people to disagree well. All of us will clash with others. Our challenge is to make sure that this does not prevent us from listening to and trying to understand one another as we live and work together.

There are two areas where reconciliation is sorely needed in our political life at present.

1 Cross-party collaboration for long-lasting solutions

First, political reconciliation between different parties and political groups is necessary so they can collaborate on facing the major challenges confronting us as a nation. Some problems are so big that no government is going to be able to solve them in one five-year parliamentary term, or even two. They need long-term – twenty years or more – plans. For that to be possible, the issues need to be taken out of the football game of politics and looked at in detail on a cross-party basis.

While there will, of course, be things that different parties disagree on within a topic area, such as housing or migration, there is usually much more agreement than we might assume from the way debates are portrayed in the media. I've pondered this a good deal, having met many MPs, peers and ministers from all political persuasions with the archbishop. Often, the main challenge is to get differing parties or groups to sit in the same room and really listen to one another.

Within our churches, there are probably people who hold the full spectrum of political opinions. You might have been having a conversation with someone and discovered (to your surprise) that you disagree quite significantly. Similarly, within Parliament, there are Christians who belong to nearly all the different parties. While those of us who work there might hold diverse views, one thing far greater than political allegiance should unite us: faith in Jesus Christ and a desire for his kingdom to be seen on earth. As Andy Flannagan from Christians in Politics puts it, we can put 'kingdom over tribe'.[5] This gives us a unique opportunity to be the bridge builders between factions, to work with other Christians across political divides and to draw our colleagues into doing this too.

The archbishop and other lords spiritual are often able to act as mediators in the House of Lords. You might not be aware that bishops sit as independent members in the so-called second chamber – they are not affiliated to any party and they take no whip. When they engage in debates and votes on legislation, they do so based on the details of the issue itself and informed by the fundamental values of Christian faith. I've noticed that the House of Lords in general – which, of course, has members of different faiths and none – works more collaboratively than the House of Commons, and the best amendments to legislation are frequently cross-party ones with peers of different political parties 'co-signing' them. Bishops are often involved with these amendments as instigators, co-signatories or supporters.

2 A hopeful response to populism

The second area where political reconciliation is sorely needed is between those who hold political power and the people they are there to serve. Before I began working for the archbishop, I spent time studying populism (populist language in particular) for an MPhil. Populism was just beginning to come to the fore in the UK, and I sensed that it would continue to have significance in the years ahead. Populism matters for two reasons. First, because the feeling of connection between people and those who hold positions of power is one of the most essential things for a healthy and functioning democracy and society, and populism can emerge when there has been a breakdown in this connection. Second, because language – how we express things – is often as important as what we are expressing. This is especially the case in politics, where there is a risk of people wanting to use words to win political battles – be they votes, elections or arguments – rather than to really solve problems or express the true state of things.

Populist language has now become dominant in the UK's mainstream political discourse and in that of many other Western nations. Calls of 'power to the people' or praise for 'the people' are expressed alongside attacks on 'the establishment', 'elites', politicians, experts, key institutions or leaders who hold power.[6]

This can be appealing because it touches on some real and legitimate feelings of concern, including a sense of a loss of connection between individuals and the political leaders who make decisions that affect them. However, populist politics often fails to deliver any real solutions to the people it purports to stand up for. Sticking plasters or fantasy solutions are offered where deeper connection and real dialogue are needed. Populism stokes antagonism, fuels an 'us and them' mentality and deepens divisions. It seeks to portray things as black and white when many areas of policy and decision-making are complex and require a nuanced approach. And it can also be dangerous because language and rhetoric have power. As Christians, we're aware that our tongues can do great good or great evil (see James 3:3–11). You only need to look at the riots in the US Capitol in January 2020 to see that the populist language of division can lead to physical violence too.

In a time where trust in politicians and public institutions has reached a low point, there is a desperate need to help to restore connection between them and the people they serve. As Christians, we have a calling to speak up for those who are marginalised and struggling, and our presence in every community across the country through the parish system means that we get to see and be involved with the lives and challenges of people in all places.

At the same time, as well as our access to our local MPs, the Church of England's unique role as the established church gives us further access to those in power – through bishops in the House of Lords and other connections with the government and Parliament. This allows us to appreciate the challenges and complexities of decision-making and the toll this can take. My prayer, as we offer support both to people and to those in power, is that we will find more ways to be a bridge between the two.

Christians in politics?

Before I finish, it's worth addressing a question some readers might have had on reading the title of this chapter: why is it included in the book at all? Perhaps you aren't sure that Christians should be engaging with or working in politics. Plenty of people have told me that, including a few friends.

A vision for hope in politics

So let me tell you why I work in this sector.

The short answer is that I feel called to it. At around the age of fourteen, I sensed that God was drawing me towards the sphere of politics and government. The longer answer is that I believe that God has a plan for the transformation of societies and nations. At the Fall, it was not only our relationship with God that was damaged but also our relationships with other people, with creation around us and with ourselves. Jesus' death and resurrection and the gift of the Holy Spirit to believers gives us the opportunity to redeem these other relationships. In Revelation 21:5, we read that God is 'making everything new' – a project that will only be completed when Jesus returns again, but one that I believe begins now – and he invites all believers to play a part, for we are carriers of his kingdom (see Luke 17:21). God, who cares about every sphere and sector of our society, calls us to be his scattered servants, to infiltrate culture and to work for the salvation and transformation of individuals in all the varied places in which we're planted.

For me, politics and government are primarily about the right ordering and flourishing of society, seeing justice done in our systems and policies, and serving and seeking the common good. As churches, we're very good at supporting people who are struggling with issues like debt, poverty and homelessness. But we must also be concerned that the laws and policies made at a national or local level aren't forcing people into these situations in the first place. As Desmond Tutu famously said, 'There comes a point where we need to stop just pulling people out of the river. We need to go upstream and find out why they're falling in.'

A vision for hope in politics

Jesus was political. He did not shy away from challenging injustice and corruption when he saw it, or from calling for people to serve one another and the common good. I firmly believe that he calls us to engage with politics too.

Sure foundation

Back in St Stephen's Hall, I'm reminded of a verse from Isaiah which I've held on to these past few years as we have faced crises and challenges as a nation: 'He will be the sure foundation for your times' (Isaiah 33:6).

God is sovereign over all – over our times, our nation, our politics. Regardless of what comes our way in the years ahead, and even if it's more shaking, God is our sure foundation. We can always look to him and have great hope.

Reflection questions

1 How would you describe your emotions towards politicians or people who hold positions of power in your area? How easy do you find it to pray for our leaders, as the Bible instructs us to do?
2 Jesus said that believers will be filled with the Spirit and release 'rivers of living water' (John 7:38). How can that shape our engagement with politics as Christians, whether it is our workspace or not?
3 How aware are you of God with you in your workplace day to day? How often do you ask him for his wisdom about the particular questions or challenges you

encounter there? For example, do you regularly pray before meetings or before drafting complex emails?
4 What might it look like if God's kingdom came into your workplace, our streets, homes and schools, and our politics? What can you do to promote that? Imagine with God and let that inspire your prayers and actions.

Hannah Spiers is an Anglican consecrated sister in the Chemin Neuf Community, a Roman Catholic community with an ecumenical vocation. The community grew out of a prayer group in Lyon, France in 1973, and currently has approximately 2,000 members in over thirty countries. The spirituality of the community is rooted both in the Ignatian tradition and in the experience of the Charismatic Renewal.

Hannah grew up in Liverpool and studied in Edinburgh before moving to London to join the first cohort of the Community of St Anselm. During her year there, she discerned a calling to community life and consecrated life. After several years in the Chemin Neuf Community in France – first for her novitiate and then serving the community's discipleship school for young adults – she was called to serve in New York City. There, she is part of the leadership team of the Community at the Crossing, an intentional ecumenical community based at the Cathedral of Saint John the Divine, inspired by the Community of St Anselm.

Bible quotations in this chapter are taken from the NIV.

7

Widening horizons

Have you ever experienced a mountaintop moment when a beautiful vista suddenly unfolds before you, and your heart swells and your lungs breathe deeper? That's how I would describe the feeling of hope.

The world of religious life and community life might conjure up certain images. It might seem rather alien. What I hope to share in this chapter is how calling and 'otherness' have widened my horizons, inspired my imagination and deepened my comprehension of how God works in the world. I will tell of the way that relating to time and simplicity has breathed fresh oxygen into my attitudes towards following Christ day by day.

As we journey, I invite you to contemplate the way that God might be speaking to you, even if the path ahead appears to be heading through unfamiliar territory. Perhaps hope might beckon as a scent on the breeze. Like the Holy Spirit, it blows wherever it chooses, but the source and the end are God. We would do well to follow our noses.

Calling and being oriented

I had never encountered anyone who was part of community or who had made a vow of celibacy until my year with the Community of St Anselm. Suddenly, I met hundreds. Speaking with them or (more often) watching them from afar, I reasoned to myself, 'Yes, I can see why this makes sense as a choice. You're more available to serve, you're more dedicated, you've no distractions ...' But when every person responded to my question, 'Why did you choose this life?' with 'Because Jesus invited me to!' I got more and more confused. I was face to face with the mystery of a way of life that seemed to demand huge changes, and yet the motivation was no more than *Jesus*.

Some time later, I had the opportunity to live the thirty-day silent retreat following the Spiritual Exercises of St Ignatius. At the beginning of the retreat, I named one of my greatest fears to my spiritual companion: that God didn't have anything specific to say to me – or if he did, it would be something hard that I would just have to 'get on with'. I also shared the perplexing reality I had encountered through my St Anselm companions: that God could call you to something based solely on who Jesus is.

What I hadn't understood, and what God graciously and mercifully revealed to me over the course of that retreat, is that Christ's call is to 'follow me'. Calling is an orientation. Following Jesus is not a one-off task; his call is continual in each moment. In the Exercises, Ignatius underlines that our purpose as God's beloved children is to glorify God. If that is the case, then there is a *universe* of possibility about what that looks like. It means that the invitation to choose relates to what God is inviting us to choose.

I understood that God was asking me to move from an attitude of 'living my life for God' – which was largely about me taking initiatives and doing good things – to an attitude of 'giving my life to God'. This was the calculated folly of the merchant who put everything aside for the pearl of great price. This surrender, experienced as baptism in the Holy Spirit, was the most important act I've ever undertaken. It brought me new hope – for my life and the lives of others – that God could be more wild, more everyday, more present in each moment than I could ever imagine. God has initiative. God holds all things. God wants us to collaborate with him in bringing his kingdom into the world – but first, through remaining with him (see John 15).

Saints and stories

I love adventure, imagination and intrigue. I remember a moment during my novitiate when the founder of my community, Father Laurent Fabre, encouraged us to read 'different kinds of stories'. Stories nourish my imagination about how God is calling us and grow my capacity to respond. Being a Christian and following Jesus is not about fitting into a mould; it is about becoming more like Christ and thus becoming who we are. Only God truly knows who that is, and you're likely to get some surprises (my calling to religious life is something I had never planned for!)

In his short and brilliant book *Luminaries*, Rowan Williams writes about the lives of twenty great Christians.

> The point is not that these are straightforwardly good and attractive folk, only that they are people who let the light through, even in lives that are sometimes flawed and compromised.[1]

A good story is one thing; the idea of 'saints' (and the risk of over-glorifying Christians) is quite another. But this perspective helped me to appreciate that saints are not perfect people who live in such a way as to set an unattainable bar for those who follow; they are ordinary people who serve an extraordinary God in all their beauty and brokenness, mistakes and successes, personal quirkiness and grace. How they died is not the question as much as why they lived. Theirs are stories we can tell to proclaim that, 'Jesus is worth it. He is really worth it.'

Through living in community, I formed relationships with people from different Christian traditions. I heard stories from my Lutheran sister about Paul Gerhardt; from my Roman Catholic sister about Mother Frances Cabrini; from my Anglican brother about Jackie Pullinger; from my Catholic Maronite brother about Saint Charbel. There's a wideness that we can miss out if we limit ourselves to our church, or our country, or 'our people'. In the creeds, we proclaim that we believe in the Communion of Saints. In the words of 'Great is Thy Faithfulness', to find 'strength for today and bright hope for tomorrow' in lives lived in the service of Jesus – not just here in this present day but across history – is a gift of the mystery of communion and community.

Common glory

The collect for the last Sunday after Trinity in the Church of England reminds us to 'read, mark, learn, and inwardly digest' the Scriptures. This is the essence of the practice of *lectio divina*, a pillar of Benedictine spirituality. Imagine if we did this with our lives, reviewing and inwardly digesting how God has been present to us today in the good, the bad, the ugly and the perplexing. Such an exercise of faith and hope trusts that whatever our day has held, God held the day. As I have come to experience, 'God doesn't waste anything'. If calling is fundamentally an orientation, that means that there is no hierarchy, no 'better' thing to choose. The only thing that counts is responding in obedience to what God asks. Any choice made for the kingdom will point beyond itself to the wisdom and folly of God.

In my community, there are married couples as well as sisters and brothers who have chosen voluntary celibacy. These states of life have their own crosses and joys, but both are equally capable of glorifying God – just as my sister as a social worker; my friend as a barista; my colleague as a security guard; my friend as an ordained chaplain; my cousin as an accountant; my neighbour as an artist; my brother as a dad, and so on. Each person in each situation is capable of glorifying God in a way that their neighbour could not.

Reflection questions

1 What is your understanding and experience of how God calls? How do you feel about God, and how might that affect your capacity to hear him today?
2 Whose are the stories that nourish you, and what have they shown you about God and how God works in the world?
3 Paul exhorts the Corinthians, 'Whatever you do, do it all for the glory of God!' (1 Corinthians 10:31). What

might be the 'whatever' in your life that you haven't considered could glorify God?

Otherness and being different

Life in community has taught me that the concept of 'otherness' is a key part of what it is to be human and a vital part of our Christian faith. We are shaped by others, perhaps more powerfully when we do not *choose* but rather *receive* them. Being together is part of how God forms us into his likeness and into his Church. Family can be a good example of this, with siblings playing a key role in helping to knock our rough edges off, teaching us about sharing and what it is to experience justice (or lack thereof!) A brother in my community often says that the Lord sends us the mission and sisters and brothers we need.

Living in community can feel like living with mirrors, where the most annoying trait in another person might actually be a trait you find in yourself and deeply dislike – or the reverse, where you feel true incomprehension as to how another being could believe a certain thing or act in a particular way. It can be humbling to discover what is hard in a relationship. Sometimes, it's a real difference in theological understanding on a particular topic; sometimes, it's which brand of tea to buy for the community kitchen.

Transparency and respect

At the Community of St Anselm, I learned that my habit of 'best face for friends, true face for back home' just didn't work anymore. It was exhausting to show up with only the parts of me I wanted to present, but it was also scary to trust that I could bring my whole self. A line from our Rule of Life helped:

> We resolve to be wholly transparent before God, who already knows us better than we know ourselves, and to grow also in transparency with one another; to share our hearts with one another, our motives, our struggles, our fears.[2]

We cannot do this in our own strength but only by leaning on God's infinite mercy. In truly welcoming the other – just as they are, just as I am – we can better see Christ.

Community life teaches me my finiteness and therefore a certain chastity and respect. There are times when I simply must allow there to be space. I struggle to see people in pain or struggle, and my first reflex is to reach out to help, to solve. But I am learning that the best thing I can do is to leave them with God. God promises, 'I will be with you.' I can pray, I can listen, I can walk alongside, but my hope and trust are in God, that God will work in them as he sees fit. Perhaps my choice to make space and time is precisely what will enable God to do a miracle more amazing than I could have imagined.

The power of relationship

What is foreign, different or strange can often unsettle me. In the 2010 BBC version of the nativity,[3] the arrival of the magi, with their foreign faces and strange clothes, at first arouses fear. But the magi's purpose is so clearly to worship Jesus that Mary and Joseph allow space for them to approach and encounter the one they had travelled to meet. This prompted me to be open to the possibility that the person who is different from me is not a threat – and they might also be bearer of good things. Unsettling and good can go together. If you trace the history of the Charismatic Renewal, you will read about the congregation of worshippers at Azusa Street. In this interracial gathering in Jim Crow America (the Jim Crow laws enforced racial segregation), 'the color line was washed away [in the blood of Jesus].'[4] This is what the Holy Spirit does; he 'allows Christians to see and enact life together, to touch, pray, and collaborate in proclaiming the gospel.'[5]

I was deeply struck when I heard Archbishop Justin Welby state during a festival in Poland that, 'Information without relationship is dangerous.' There is a difference between knowing and knowing about. Growing up, I more or less unconsciously nurtured an image of Roman Catholics as those who recited prayers without meaning them, worshipped Mary and blindly obeyed the Pope. It was only through sharing daily life with Roman Catholics that I started to encounter them as people who loved Jesus (more than me, would you believe?) and were committed to the Church, and they were rather unsettlingly vulnerable about it all.

To give another example, years of living in the UK and hearing background grumbling about 'foreigners taking our jobs' had fostered in me a wary mistrust of 'them'.

Widening horizons

When I actually found myself in an unfamiliar country – meeting real flesh-and-blood people, listening to their stories and struggles and receiving their hospitality – something in me shifted. Why had I not grasped before that there are individual lives behind each fact and figure?

A friend told me about the programme she coordinates in the US, which brings together host families and international students. One such family welcomed a Palestinian student several years ago. The moment the Gaza–Israel conflict started on 7 October 2023, she received a call from the family: 'Is Jason ok?' They did not know about a situation; they knew someone. Information without relationship increases the risk that we end up in echo chambers and go around making unfounded assumptions. Relationships disarm. When reciprocity and vulnerability are involved, walls begin to crumble, though some might need to be taken down brick by brick.

The most important experience of 'other' is, of course, God himself. God remains a mystery, yet a mystery we are always understanding more. The Lord's Prayer, through which we pray for God's kingdom to come and will to be done, is all about 'otherness'. I am invited to surrender to how God and others will form and shape me according to God's design and purpose.

Each member of my community makes a yearly retreat – and God shows up every time, never wasting an opportunity to bring about change and conversion, to heal and renew. I've seen this across generations, across cultures, across experiences, and it's a source of profound hope for me. 'He who began a work in you will carry it on to completion'

(Philippians 1:6). What good news! The journey is never finished. God continues to create.

Reflection questions

1 Who are the people in your life who you have received rather than chosen, and how have they shaped you?
2 When has the choice to trust or be vulnerable been life giving?
3 Have you experienced a change of opinion or feelings towards a person or topic? What was the reason for this?
4 How has God surprised you in your life?

Time and being present

The default way that I look at time is as a possession: I spend time, I save time, I covet time. This attitude can seep into my spiritual life as well, when time with God becomes an opportunity to make efficient progress. Leaving behind a busy life in Edinburgh for my year at the Community of St Anselm, I was suddenly confronted with a lot of time, especially for prayer: a whole hour in the morning for personal prayer; another hour in the evening for silent prayer; sessions of communal prayer; weekly desert days and regular retreats. My excitement about my impending meteoric spiritual advancement quickly turned to disillusionment as the weeks passed and I felt that very little had changed. But why? A fellow member lent me a book by the Jesuit Jean-Pierre de Caussade, and his words began to bring me understanding:

God was holy in the beginning, he is holy now, he will always be holy, there are no moments that are not filled with his infinite holiness – therefore, there are none that we should not honour.[6]

I had had a false equation in my head: more clock time spent with God would equal more spiritual progress. But, if every moment is an opportunity of revelation of God and encounter with him, my challenge is not to spend more time with God but to inhabit the present moment where God is already to be found. I can experience the fullness of God right here and now, and instead of plotting my own spiritual progress, allow that encounter to form my actions.

Obedience to time

Jesus himself spent thirty years in Nazareth. It was a hidden life, a daily life.[7] He was obedient to time and to what he received from the Father. As we imitate Christ, we also journey from step to step, from conversion to conversion. Not everything can or will be resolved today. The model of commitment in religious communities embodies this. Most start with a period of novitiate (typically between one and two years), then temporary vows (around three years) and finally life commitment. There is wisdom in this model, and it has helped me to understand more generally what it is to say 'yes' to God. As I pass through different seasons of life, I grow in my understanding of who God is and how God calls me, and each 'yes' becomes a truer and truer 'yes'. This is good news – I am a work in progress, and things take time. 'There are some things that only ten years will teach you,' remarked a wise friend recently. To surrender to time is an act of deep trust and hope.

Eternity and the present

The way we choose to relate to time can be radically evangelistic. C. S. Lewis's Screwtape explains how God would have us 'continually concerned either with eternity (which means being concerned with Him) or with the Present'.[8] I often visit a monastery in Hudson Valley in New York where the brothers meet five times a day in the chapel to pray together. This might seem somewhat disruptive to the rhythm of the day, but that's the whole point – being interrupted in what you're doing to be present to eternity.

We are in the 'already here' and the 'not yet'. We are saved, and we are being saved. This can be embodied through certain vows. For example, marriage points to the 'already here' of the love and commitment of Christ to his Church, and consecrated celibacy points to the hope of the 'not yet' of the eternal kingdom to come, where truly 'God alone suffices'.[9] Choosing consecrated life is an act of hope: I am willing to stake my life on the fact that Jesus is real, his promises are everlasting and this earthly life is not all there is.

Our attitude to time can also be embodied in the simplest everyday actions. A powerful way of loving someone today is to listen to them. Heart to Heart is one of the most important ministries of the young adult festival run by my community. Put simply, it is a service of listening in which pairs of brothers and sisters will make themselves available to anyone who wants to talk. Sometimes, you sit and wait for an hour and no one comes. But this is not wasted time, because in order for someone to be ready to talk, they have to see someone ready to listen. Listening requires being present, making space, taking time and not hurrying. This is not easy – indeed, it is costly. But I've become convinced that it's worth the effort. Journeying with the same people through time allows me to witness the transformation that only God can bring about. Sharing rhythms of labour and rest, and celebrating different calendars, reminds me that there is another music I can dance to. It reminds me that I am free to choose whether I run or walk.

Reflection questions

1 How do you feel about time?
2 What are the conditions that enable you to be present to God? How often are they a reality for you?
3 'There are some things that only ten years will teach you.' What is an example of this in your life?
4 What is your reaction to Jesus' thirty 'hidden' years in Nazareth?

Simplicity and being people of commitment

In a team meeting preparing for the first cohort of the Community at the Crossing, we remarked to one another that fewer had applied than we had hoped for. We were looking at a group of around a dozen. One of the brothers noted dryly, 'Yes, because Jesus didn't achieve much with twelve people.'

Simplicity teaches us to embrace small beginnings and to be content with what we have. The Covid-19 pandemic was both universal and diversely experienced, but one thing I think we all learned was to re-appreciate the smallest things – such as a hug, the ability to travel or singing together.

A wise priest I work with in New York has a note stuck to her computer screen: 'Even the smallest amount of engagement is better than avoidance.' Whether situations feel huge and overwhelming, hopeless or hopeful, the call is the same: to remain with Jesus. Choosing what is simple does not mean the same as choosing what is easy. Simplicity can usher in the power and complexity of God. The Alpha course consists largely of conversation and food, and yet God works remarkable things in the lives of those who attend. The Spiritual Exercises have remained the same for centuries, and yet people – across countries, cultures and generations – have been and continue to be transformed. Putting together a weekend for young adults recently, we realised that the group didn't want impressive content; they wanted relationship. We spent a weekend in prayer, sharing in small groups, eating together and walking in the countryside. The depth of what that space allowed was astounding.

Open hands

Have you heard the story of how to catch a monkey? Take a bottle with a neck just wide enough for a monkey to fit its empty hand through, fill it with food and tie it to a tree. As soon as the monkey reaches in and grabs a handful of food, he will no longer be able to retract his hand because his fist is too wide. He could get free if he only let go of the food. Whether this story is accurate or not, I think that it's a poignant image. I can be enslaved by what I hold on to, but I am free when I choose to open my hands. I've seen this paradox play out time and time again. There is something holy and humbling about days spent waiting for an airline to deliver your lost bag. It can birth a surprising creativity in how you manage your one t-shirt and inspire generosity in your neighbour who sees (or smells) you without toothpaste. I've been deeply impacted by the generosity of different church communities where I grew up in Liverpool. Often, it was the least well-off people who made sure that no corner shop order was forgotten and no birthday went without a celebration. Generosity is an attitude of the heart.

The everyday 'yes'

As Jesus followers, the simplicity of daily life shapes and equips us to respond to the world. Think of how a stone is moulded by being underneath a waterfall. There is no strain on the stone's part; simply a remaining. Simplicity invites us to trust the everyday rather than hankering after remarkable results. If what you are doing is real and in response to God's call, then it is worthwhile.

Definitive commitments are undertaken with the pronouncing of vows, but every married couple will tell you that you only stay married through the everyday choices you make. This is one of the most remarkable examples of community and simplicity. I have been surprised (but pleasantly so) about how important the presence of married couples in my community and family have been for my own spiritual growth. As a single consecrated sister, my imagination can conjure up a rich, escapist fantasies: 'This way of life is hard, it would be so much easier if I were married.' But you cannot sustain a grass-is-greener mindset when you are face to face with the reality. While it might be easier to take refuge in the imaginary than to confront the real poverty of my situation, true strength comes from acknowledging and learning from what I see around me – overwhelming as it might feel that there is no perfect state of life, no situation free of difficulty.

Today, with 'cancel anytime' deals easily available, the idea of commitment can seem very alien. We need models of lifelong commitment to encourage us; we need people who promise, 'for better, for worse,' and base their choices not on the emotion of the moment but on something deeper. Relationships of commitment, where we learn mutual submission and the art of putting others first, both transform us and are a sign to the world that commitment is possible. I see this desire to experience something radical all around me – in the meteoric rise and popularity of boot camps and diet challenges; in the New York church where the most popular prayer room session is the one that starts at 6 a.m.; in the intentional community in California that experienced a rise in membership when they *increased* the time commitment.

To journey with

Commitment means time. Over the years, different groups at Chemin Neuf have sprung up organically when brothers and sisters have wanted to study matters that affected them personally in the company of others. Topics have included the effects of communism in Eastern Europe, the Jewish roots of Christianity, and the history and repercussions of slavery (particularly in places such as Brazil, Mauritius, Guadeloupe and Martinique). As those in the groups committed to working through these complex questions, they committed to one another. Such commitment enables us to surrender to time and to the journey. We are pilgrims, not competitively productive shift workers. There are no shortcuts where truth and reconciliation are concerned. I can feel overwhelmed by the complexity of life, but to know that there are people dedicated to working together fills me with hope. Christ moves one person at a time.

In the book *The Vowed Life*, the Littlemore Group underlines that baptism is the first and key commitment or vow in our life as Christians. Any other vow follows from there – ordination, marriage, religious …[10] They all have their source and sense in the death and resurrection of Christ.

One of the most important things I have learned over the past few years is that vows of poverty, chastity and obedience are orientations for every Christian. We are called to imitate the self-emptying of Jesus as Paul describes it in Philippians 2 – a journey of descent in which Jesus rejected wealth, appearance and power (see Luke 4) by choosing poverty, chastity and obedience.

This is not easy, and it is impossible to do alone. But when we commit with God, God commits with us. God is not a 'let's see how you do' God but an 'I will betroth you to me for ever' one (Hosea 2). God gives us community and companionship to strengthen us in our commitment to journey with and towards him.

Looking back at the months before I joined the St Anselm Community, I see that they were marked by paradox. I was experiencing satisfaction and joy in my walk with Jesus, yet I had an ineffable hunger for more. Today, my horizons have widened beyond what I would have dreamed possible thanks to the people who have embodied previously unfamiliar ways of life.

Finding God in all things, embracing diversity, inhabiting the present moment, choosing the sacrifice of simplicity, daring to commit – these are treasures hidden in plain sight. They are 'not too difficult ... or beyond your reach' (Deuteronomy 30:11). 'Hope that is seen is no hope at all. Who hopes for what they already have?' (Romans 8.24). Hope starts by living it, in whichever context and daily life is ours. Then, in humility and assurance, we can offer them as gifts to the world.

Reflection questions

1 What is the small beginning in your life today that you need to take care of or pay attention to?
2 Where have you seen instances of generosity? What have you learned through them?

3 What is an everyday 'yes' that you make, and what impact do you see it have?
4 How has community enabled you to hold or deepen a commitment?

Dr Belle Tindall writes and curates stories for Seen & Unseen and hosts conversations for its Re-enchanting podcast at the Centre for Cultural Witness. She holds a doctorate in biblical studies, specialising in Jesus' interactions with women, Jewish-Christian relations in the New Testament and ancient media culture.

Bible quotations in this chapter are taken from the NIV.

8

A beautiful and messy awakening

> I had thought that going into space would be the ultimate catharsis of that connection I had been looking for between all living things – that being *up there* would be the next beautiful step to understanding the harmony of the universe ... My trip to space was supposed to be a celebration; instead, it felt like a funeral.[1]

Those words are quite something, aren't they?

They were written by the Canadian actor William Shatner. You might know him as Captain James T. Kirk, his intergalactic alter-ego. He's reflecting on the ten minutes he spent in space in 2021, an adventure that was ninety years in the making. But what he looked for, he didn't find. What he assumed would bring him joy somehow brought him grief.

As I pondered the magnitude of Shatner's reflections, a phrase came to my mind. It's not my own – it was written in AD 397, by St Augustine of Hippo – but it goes like this: 'You have made us, O Lord, for yourself, and our hearts are restless until they find their rest in you.'

A beautiful and messy awakening

I believe this to be completely and utterly true – true of me, true of you, true of every single one of us. I believe that we were made, wonderfully and fearfully, in the image of the one who did the making. I believe that he made us for himself, to glorify him and enjoy him forever. And, what's more, I believe that our souls know it, even if they don't *know* they know it. There's an itch we can't seem to scratch, a hunger we can't seem to satisfy, a desire so deep we struggle to even put words to it. We were made for God. No one is exempt. No one is disqualified. And so, just as Augustine notices, our 'hearts are restless'.

It seems to me that William Shatner boarded a spacecraft assuming that his restless heart would find its rest up there. But it didn't, and that sums up our cultural moment pretty well.

Sticking with the space metaphor for just a moment longer, I'm seeing countless people on their way 'up'. They're seeking and striving, going after anything they can to satisfy their deepest longings. They're consoling their restless hearts, telling themselves that if they could just achieve this, go there, experience that, gain those, meet them, then they would find their rest. I'm also seeing plenty of other people on their way back 'down' again, disillusioned, defeated and confused because it – whatever *it* was for them – simply didn't work. It was supposed to feel like a celebration but somehow felt like a funeral.

This cultural moment, with all the seeking and striving, has a touch of Psalm 121 about it: 'I lift up my eyes to the mountains – where does my help come from?' (Psalm 121:1).

- Where does my worth come from?
- Where does my meaning come from?
- Where does my rest come from?

It's interesting, after decades of New Atheism ruling the roost, that we're even still asking such questions. Apparently, neither Richard Dawkins's best-selling books nor his double-decker buses with the message 'There's probably no God. Now stop worrying and enjoy your life' emblazoned across them had the desired effect. We're still 'lifting our eyes', still searching, still seeking. It doesn't seem to be something we can opt out of. Maybe that is, in itself, a kind of marker of the truth of God's existence. But it's like we're perpetually stuck on the first verse of Psalm 121, and we're spiralling.

So here's the truly exciting part: God appears to be showing up and moving people into the truth of the second line of the Psalm, the one that reads, 'My help [or worth, meaning, or rest] comes from the LORD, the Maker of heaven and earth' (Psalm 121:2). I've noticed that he appears to be interrupting people as they're on the way 'up' and on their way back 'down'.

'What *is* going on with Christianity?'

While I'm reluctant to over-hypothesise, over-define or over-simplify what God is up to in this cultural moment (as, truly, only time will tell), I can't help but feel that he's up to *something*. I, for one, am incredibly excited about it. I don't expect you to agree with me quite yet; I imagine that

A beautiful and messy awakening

I have a little winning over to do, some sort of evidence to provide.

That's fine. I came prepared.

In June 2019, grime artist and all-round icon Stormzy headlined Glastonbury festival's iconic Pyramid Stage. In front of the 200,000 people standing before him, and a further one million people watching live from their homes, Stormzy declared that he was, 'Going to give God all the glory.' He proceeded to pray and worship his way through his history-making headline set.

The same year, renowned mythologist Dr Martin Shaw decided to do a 101-day wild vigil in Dartmoor. On the very last night, he prayed. While praying, he looked up and saw something utterly unexplainable, something 'properly Old Testament'. And that was it. After a night of dancing, a number of other 'odd' experiences, and eighteen months of deep pondering, he was able to say, 'I went into the woods to be wedded to the wild and I came out wedded to Christ.'[2]

In 2022, Australian rock maestro Nick Cave released a book (in collaboration with his friend, journalist and critic Sean O'Hagan) entitled *Faith, Hope and Carnage*. This book tells the story of Cave's inner life: battles with a heroin addiction, the tragic death of his teenage son, the agony and ecstasy of the creative process, and God. Throughout the book, he speaks powerfully, poetically and intimately about his journey back into the arms of God. He later released a critically acclaimed album and went on a widely praised tour, both entitled 'Wild God', as he continued to tell the story of how he found faith and hope even in the midst of carnage.

A beautiful and messy awakening

In early 2023, the mainstream media was bewildered by what was happening in a university chapel in Asbury, a rural town in Kentucky. The *New York Times* headline called what was occurring there 'Woodstock for Christians', explaining how what had started as a run-of-the-mill gathering of twenty(ish) students had somehow become a gathering of over 50,000 people from all over the world. It was the service that didn't end. Hours turned into days, which turned into weeks as news spread across the world of a spiritual outpouring happening in a modest chapel that was inexplicably bursting at the seams. The immense online attention it garnered led *The Atlantic* to refer to that sixteen-day-long service as the first ever 'viral revival'.[3]

In 2024, former champion of New Atheism Ayaan Hirsi Ali sat on a stage and explained why she was now a Christian to a rather stunned Richard Dawkins. She told him, 'What has happened to me is that I have accepted that there is something ... the God who turned me around ... Like you, I used to mock faith in general, and probably Christianity in particular, but I don't do that anymore.'[4]

Fascinating, isn't it?

A journalist called me recently, totally out of the blue. She wasn't a Christian, nor did she work for a Christian publication, but she approached me with one simple question: 'What on earth is going on with Christianity at the moment?'

I assumed that she was referencing the things I mentioned above – Stormzy praying on the most iconic stage in the world or Ayaan Hirsi Ali delivering a verbal sucker punch to Richard Dawkins – so I started chatting my way through this list of cultural anecdotes.

A beautiful and messy awakening

'Yes, yes, yes. That's all very interesting,' she said. 'But I'm asking because, whatever's happening, it's happening in my family.'

And that, quite rightly, shut me up.

She proceeded to tell me about family members and friends of hers who were becoming Christians, seemingly out of nowhere, many of them having spent their lives as firm atheists. Then, as her professional walls came inching down, she told me that she was also feeling unexplainable cravings: a strong pull to step into a church, a bizarre and unfamiliar desire to read the Bible, a new fascination with the supernatural. I suppose that she was experiencing what Augustine diagnosed: a 'restless heart'. And so, she asked me again, 'Tell me, what is happening?'

I had no nice, neat, sloganised answer for her, just as I have none for you.[5] If anything, I left the conversation asking myself (and God) the very same question: what *is* going on? My conversation with that curious journalist made me realise something: I had spent so much time gazing into the limelight – studying the God-stories that were making the news, tracking the so-called viral testimonies – that I hadn't done what she had done. I hadn't looked at my own community: my friends, my family, my neighbours. So I began to.

She was right. Things are rumbling there too.

Since that conversation, I've had impromptu conversations about God with people on the street – and trust me, I'm no natural evangelist. I did not, could not and would not make those conversations happen on my own.

I've had messages from people I was in school with back home in rural west Wales who have become Christians, a number of them coming out of a heavy reliance on psychedelic drugs.

Last summer, I preached at my friend's wedding. She's a Christian and her (now) husband is not, so it was a very mixed room. Again, not being a natural evangelist, I was more than a little nervous. But, as a result of my (mediocre) preach, I spent the entire day answering the guests' endless questions about Jesus. The next day, I woke up to a message from the photographer asking about church.

And here's the really interesting thing about all of that, this second category of people: they don't know about what happened in Asbury in 2023, and they don't care about the infamous Hirsi Ali U-turn of 2024. It's not like they've been looking out for cultural cues that Christianity is the 'in thing' again. The way God is showing up and changing their lives is happening completely independently of those things. And so, when all of this is happening at the same time, you have to pause and wonder. Is something shifting? Is the spirit of God doing a new thing?

I think that he might just be.

Are we ready?

The first thing I want you to feel when you read these stories – and ponder your own versions of them – is hope. Our great and gracious God is up to something beautiful in this cultural moment. I'm certain of it. The evidence is all over the place. Where, at times, it has felt like we've been wading through some kind of secular wasteland, blown about and battered by the angry winds of rigid atheism and general disenchantment, change appears to be afoot. Even if we can't quite explain it, even if it flies in the face of news reports and census data, even if it's made complicated by imperfect humans, God is doing something in this cultural moment, and the little of it that we can see should cause us to thank him and simply ask for more of it.

Call me naive, but I'm excited.

I'm also wondering, 'Are we ready?' If God said a simple, 'OK,' to our prayer for more, would we be ready for it? If what I (and many others) perceive to be happening is truly happening – if the soil of peoples' hearts is becoming soft again, more porous and more ready to absorb the truth of the gospel – are we ready? Because, if this is what's happening in our cultural context, it will require something a little different from us. It will require us to shift out of survival mode and move beyond a scarcity mindset. It will require us to steward the abundance well.

I have two (initial) thoughts on how we can do that, and there's a perfect blueprint of both of them in Acts 17:16–34. In this chunk of the Bible, we see Paul arrive in Athens, the place where ideas take root and meaning is made. This is the cultural epicentre of the Graeco-Roman world. As a result of preaching about Jesus in synagogues and on street corners, he's thrown before the Areopagus, a culture-making council in every kind of way, and then things get *really* interesting.

Bless the mess

Let's kick off with Paul's first words: 'People of Athens! I see that in every way you are very religious' (Acts 17:22). As far as openers go, it's a bold one.

Last summer, I went to Glastonbury festival. I reckon you would only need to spend about three minutes at that iconic farm before you could stand in the middle of it and confidently declare, 'People of Glastonbury! I see that in every way you are very religious.' There's a whole section of the festival called The Healing Fields where every spiritual experience you could imagine is available to you. There are social justice campaigns, political activism and communal experiences. In 2024, Coldplay's Chris Martin headlined with the words 'God is Love' written on his arm. The whole thing, if you think about it, is 200,000 people pausing their lives and paying an extortionate price (though, admittedly, not as much as William Shatner paid to go to space) to seek out awe, wonder and transcendence. 'Secular musical festival' my foot. Nothing has changed. We – the good old human race – always have been and always will be 'religious' in every kind of way.

Why? Because we were made by and for God. There's no escaping that.

Paul goes on: 'I even found an alter with this inscription: TO AN UNKNOWN GOD' (Acts 17:23). I reckon that's polite Paul-speak for, 'But you still haven't found what you're looking for, have you?' It has a feel of that U2 song about it, don't you think?

> I have climbed highest mountains
> I have run through the fields
> Only to be with you
> Only to be with you
> I have run, I have crawled
> I have scaled these city walls
> These city walls
> Only to be with you
> But I still haven't found what I'm looking for[6]

Those lyrics, written by an Irish rockstar in the twentieth century, could have easily been written by an Athenian in the first century, by Augustine in the fourth century or by a Glastonbury-goer in the twenty-first century. To long for the one who made us for himself is part of what it means to be human. So here's the first piece of advice I'm taking from Paul when it comes to how we can best engage with this particular cultural moment: don't dismiss or demonise it. I'd shout this from the rooftops if I could.

As I've mentioned – and as you'll know well – people are looking here, there and everywhere for the thing(s) that will satisfy their deepest longings and answer their innermost questions. We, the Church, have a tendency to do one of two things. We laugh at it all, roll our eyes and dismiss the people who are looking in places we don't agree with or believe in. Or, perhaps even more damagingly, we demonise them for it. There are people who charge up their crystals in the sunlight, have their tarot cards read, dabble in alternative healing methods, swear by sound baths, live according to their lunar identities, meditate and manifest

A beautiful and messy awakening

(all of which is becoming increasingly common, by the way), and we act as if they are either (a) just plain silly, or (b) knowingly acting in direct defiance of the God who made them for himself.

But here's the thing: what if they're neither of those things? What if the vast majority of people are not – I repeat, *not* – actively endeavouring to hurt God by looking and going elsewhere? What if they just know that they were made for something more, and they're desperately searching for what that 'more' might be?

Culture, in and of itself, is not an enemy. We don't have to be so suspicious of it. Notice that Paul has a real and generous curiosity about the Athenian cultural climate. He sees what lies at the heart of it all. It's like he can hear the cultural heart-cries underlying all the noise. He even quotes two Athenian poets in his speech about Jesus ('As some of your own poets have said ...' (Acts 17:28)), using their words to explain his saviour.

What a radically honouring tactic. Paul arrives in Athens and decides to read the room through the lens of grace, always aware that the truest thing about every person there is that they were made for God, so they're probably, in a myriad of imperfect ways, seeking him out.

We could learn a lot from that. At least, I know that I could.

I'm not saying that we can't be concerned or cautious. On the contrary, as soon as Paul sets foot in Athens, he's 'greatly distressed to see that the city is full of idols' (Acts 17:16). It's OK for us to be distressed at all the wrong places people are looking and all the wrong things they're worshipping. It's right that we get distressed at the forces (societal and spiritual) manipulating people into finding their rest outside of God. But distress at the situation doesn't have to become demonisation of the people.

Clinical psychologist and Associate Professor Dr Roger Bretherton made this observation:

> I do think our culture is desperately running out of steam and many people are looking for something that truly settles their minds and satisfies their hearts. My feeling is that we could be heading towards a great and messy spiritual awakening.

Let's not demonise people for what's actually the truest thing about them, even if it's leading them in some messy directions. Instead, we could try praying into it, asking something like, 'Lord, in your wild grace, would you bless the mess?'

Going for bold

I noticed something else in Acts 17: there's both a boldness to Paul's speech and a bullseye right at the heart of it.

First, let's take a little look at his boldness.

Paul has been thrown in front of a bunch of people who have got listening to the latest ideas and philosophies down to a fine art, so it makes sense that that's exactly what they think Paul has to offer them: a new idea or a fresh theory. But Paul is having none of that. Notice how he introduces God as 'the God who made the world and everything in it

A beautiful and messy awakening

… he himself gives everyone life and breath and everything else' (Acts 17:24–25). There's nothing deeper or truer than the message Paul has to offer, and he wants the Athenians to know it. Theologian C. Kavin Rowe says, 'Bluntly put, it can scarcely get older than this: the God about whom Paul speaks created the world in which Athens exists.'[7]

We don't have some good news to share, we have *the* good news. We don't have an option to offer people, we have *the* option. The only true option, the only one there ever was and the only one there ever will be. He was the same yesterday, today and forever. He is still the one who gives everyone life, breath and everything else. He is still the one who made us for himself. To borrow, and then tweak, Rowe's words, the God about whom Paul (and we) speak created the world in which William Shatner's spacecraft and Glastonbury's Healing Fields exist. This is not the time for us to lose our confidence; we must humbly but boldly insist that Jesus is *it*. He is the truest thing there is. He is the realest thing we could ever know. He's the only one who can satisfy.

Which leads me to the bullseye at the heart of Paul's bold speech. It's Jesus. Shocking, I know.

It makes sense. Jesus is the way, the truth and the life, right? He's the beginning, the middle and the end of our message. I know that we know this. But it's surprising how easy it is to forget, particularly when trying to witness to a culture that hasn't quite caught on.

May I get sassy for just a moment? I'm a little bit tired of people calling Christianity a political or societal 'good', and increasingly confused when I hear people call Jesus an

A beautiful and messy awakening

'archetype' or God 'the highest value'. Christianity has only ever been 'useful', as I hear it called these days, because people have believed it to be true and lived their lives in radical accordance. You can't have the fruit without the tree, there's no such thing as a purely 'cultural Christian' and it's weird that that's becoming a phrase. A 'culture-making Christian', sure – that was the precise reputation of the early church as they sought to live like Jesus in all kinds of bold and creative ways. It's my hope that it would become our reputation once again. But Christianity being approached as nothing more than a set of values? No, no, no.

When people think like that, they're thinking like the Athenians.

Our message has a name and scars on his hands. Our message became flesh and dwelt among us. Our message exited his own grave. Our message is Jesus.

Everything we are is a response to his life, death and resurrection. Without him, we really have nothing to say. People are desperate for rest, and they'll find it in Jesus. They're craving meaning, and they'll find it in Jesus. They're searching for peace, and – you guessed it – they'll find it in Jesus. He is the invitation we have to give. As Chris Russell reminds us, he is 'all-involving, all-consuming, all-encompassing, all-freeing'.[8] If we're trying to offer people a spiritual experience, a political solution or a way of life, we're selling them way too short.

What this cultural moment, and the people dwelling within it, need is to know that every spiritual longing, every soul-level desire is real and true, and there's one name in which they all find their fulfilment. And, what's more, we can gladly introduce them to the one who holds that name. They need to be told, again and again and again, that God aches for them even more than they ache for him.

They have been made by and for God, and their hearts will stay restless until they find their rest in him. So let's continue to shout it from the Pyramid Stage, write it in books, and sing it until the *New York Times* notices.

God is up to something. At least, that's my proposition. I think that we're in for a bright and wild ride, and I'm excited about it. How about you?

Reflection questions

1 Think of the people in your life – friends, colleagues, neighbours, family members. Which places do they go to in an attempt to soothe their 'restless hearts'?
2 Let's get even more personal: which places do you tend to go to when your heart is feeling restless?
3 I've listed a few examples of where I see God doing something a little exciting, popping up where I wasn't expecting him to. Now, it's over to you. Do you have any examples – cultural or local – where God has shown up in an unexpected place?
4 Thinking about Paul's iconic speech at the Areopagus, is there anything else he says or does that we can learn from and put to use in this cultural moment?

Toby Lewis Thomas is an Anglican priest serving as the Mission Enabler for Hackney and Islington, where he works alongside churches to support the growth of new worshipping communities. His journey into ministry began in Hackney and Shoreditch, East London.

Before stepping into church leadership, Toby spent over a decade in the creative industries, running a photography and directing agency. Later, he transitioned to the role of Global Creative Director at Alpha International, bringing his passion for storytelling and community into his work.

Toby grew up in the New Forest and has called London home for the past fourteen years.

Bible quotations in this chapter are taken from the NIV.

9

The radical grace of God

At some point in every person's life, whether through a silent plea or a shout of joy in an empty room, I am convinced that each of us utters a prayer. Gregory the Great spoke about *compunctio*, the holy pain, 'the grief somebody feels when faced with that which is most beautiful. This bittersweet experience stems from human homelessness in an imperfect world.'[1]

It is this beauty, this ache, that draws us to ponder God and acknowledge that there is something missing – a space to be filled or a question to be answered. It is the same restlessness Augustine refers to when he says, 'Our hearts are restless until they find rest in you.' Rolheiser writes, 'Spirituality is, ultimately, about what we do with that desire. What we do with our longings, both in terms of handling the pain and the hope they bring us, that is our spirituality.'[2]

For most of my life, I carried with me a scepticism about faith – or at least a suspicion of the institution of the Church. My childhood memories of my Church of England school are mostly of dull daily assemblies and regular trips to the parish church. These visits were marked by my constant inability to sit still and recurrent scolding – especially during Christmas, when I would eat the sweets from my Christingle too early.

The radical grace of God

The church, with its rigid structure, seemed designed to suppress rather than embrace me. Yet during my college years, as I grappled with the disruptive nature of my ADHD and the overwhelming pressures of life, I found myself strangely drawn back. I would set out from Brockenhurst College, wander through a nearby village, cross a little brook and then spend time in the echoing nave of a small parish church.

As sunlight filtered through the stained-glass windows and cast jewel-toned patterns on the stone under my feet, I discovered my form of prayer. It was surrender, an acknowledgement that something larger than myself was present, a sense that I was being held by an unseen force. Prayer was not just an obligation imposed by religion but an invitation extended by life itself, an invitation to a conversation with the one who holds it all together.

> Come to me, all you who are weary and burdened, and I will give you rest. Take my yoke upon you and learn from me, for I am gentle and humble in heart, and you will find rest for your souls. For my yoke is easy and my burden is light.
> (Matthew 11:28–30)

Last autumn, a few friends and I embarked on a unique venture right in the heart of a bustling market street in central London, a place alive with crowded bars and restaurants. Carrying lanterns and working with the local parish church, we gently invited passers-by to step inside a quiet, sacred space.

The radical grace of God

It was magical to witness the transformation as people crossed the threshold. Faces lit up as they entered the candlelit church, the air thick with the scent of incense. In line with the Catholic tradition, the sacrament was displayed on the altar. We guided each individual to the altar rail and handed them a candle of their own. They were invited to light it, say a prayer and, if they wished, write their prayers on a piece of paper or speak with someone at the back of the room who was ready to pray with them.

Within a couple of hours, 180 strangers had wandered in from the street. Drawn from the chaos of the city in search of a moment of peace and connection, some found an opportunity to share in honest questioning and conversation. Others, in tears, experienced a sense of coming home.

That moving night spoke to me powerfully of God's desire to move in our lives. As the pastor Jon Tyson observes, 'God comes where he is wanted'.[3] This echoes the words of Jesus: 'Ask and it will be given to you; seek and you will find; knock and the door will be opened to you' (Matthew 7:7).

If we create space for God, he will fill it. God is not indifferent to our existence; rather, his profound desire is to dwell with us, and we invite his presence to transform and enrich our lives through our openness and intentionality.

For those outside of the church, discovering faith can be like uncovering a hidden world that has existed all along beside the familiar one. If – like me – you became a

Christian later in life, those first few years were probably filled with excitement and a profound sense of wonder. You were journeying into the unknown, and every step could reveal something previously unseen.

But what about when we have walked this path for many years? Then the experience can be rather different. The fresh insights that once sparked joy and awe can lose their lustre. Prayer, instead of feeling alive and life giving, can fade into routine. If we are honest, we can all encounter moments when we simply feel stuck in our spiritual practice, all vibrancy gone.

These moments of spiritual dryness can make us believe that we are failing, but in fact they offer us an opportunity to rediscover the riches that once captivated us. We are being called to embrace the mystery of faith with fresh eyes and an open heart, to renew our commitment to the journey and to seek out new ways of connecting with God. In such seasons, it is good to remember that growing to spiritual maturity is the work of a lifetime.

In reflecting on prayer in this chapter, I would like to suggest that we begin again with something simple. Prayer can take many forms – including adoration, confession, intercession, petition and thanksgiving – yet it does not always require words. Sometimes, it is just about being present, opening oneself to the possibility of connection with the divine. Psalm 46 reminds us of a form of adoration that comes with speechlessness: 'Be still, and know that I am God' (Psalm 46:10).

As a minister in the church, I must admit that I often overcomplicate prayer (paradoxically) by reducing it to less than it truly is. I regard it as a task or a transaction, something to be accomplished rather than experienced. Or I let it become overly traditional, a routine in which I recite words without truly being moved by the one I am speaking to.

I felt deeply convicted when I read the words of Strahan Coleman in his book *Beholding*:

> My default approach to prayer was as a place to pass important information and requests between God and me, rather than seeing it as a place to simply stare at the mystery of God. To waste time on and with Him.[4]

Those words lingered in my mind, challenging my approach and reminding me of prayer's true purpose, which is beautifully encapsulated in the Westminster Catechism: 'Man's chief end is to glorify God, and to enjoy Him forever.'

This is the essence of prayer. It is not merely a tool for communication or a means to an end but a place where we glorify God by simply being in his presence: 'In the space of beholding prayer, we are allowed to not feel anything and still consider our time as best spent.'[5]

An observation

The practice of retreating to a quiet space for reflection and prayer is a tradition set by Jesus himself and modelled in his own spiritual life. Throughout the gospels, we frequently see him seeking solitude for prayer and communion with God, withdrawing from the crowds to try to find moments to be alone with his Father:

> Very early in the morning, while it was still dark, Jesus got up, left the house and went off to a solitary place, where he prayed.
> (Mark 1:35)

> But Jesus often withdrew to lonely places and prayed.
> (Luke 5:16)

I often wonder what these moments were like for Jesus. Was it akin to having a private phone call, where you need to leave the room to participate in a real heart-to-heart? We know that Jesus always treasured being in his Father's presence; he was still a child when he told his parents, 'I had to be in my Father's house' (Luke 2:49).

These moments of solitude would also be times when Jesus received instruction and guidance – 'he can only do what he sees his Father doing' (John 5:19) – as we ourselves might sometimes do.

In our busy lives, it is easy to overlook the importance of solitude and reflection. But Jesus' example teaches us that taking time to retreat and pray is essential for maintaining a deep and meaningful connection with our Creator. I believe that it is also the starting point for rekindling a relationship with God.

The day I wrote these words, there was something of a replay of my own story.

A gentle stranger arrived at the door of the church where I am now an assistant priest and asked if he could come inside. Jokingly, I replied, 'Come on in, have a sing, lie down on the floor. You're most welcome.' To my surprise, he walked up to the chancel, lay down on the floor, gazed up at the high ceiling and let out a sigh as if he had just set down a heavy burden. He had come seeking answers, longing for a sense of peace and purpose in the middle of a hectic, ever-changing world.

I have spent some time reflecting on the foundation of a vibrant prayer life, and I believe that there are three essential elements: time, place and words.

Time: making time to be interrupted for holy things

In our relentless pursuit of productivity, the idea of being interrupted by sacred moments feels almost alarming. Yet these 'holy interruptions' are precisely what our souls crave. They invite us to pause, step outside of the ceaseless rhythm of our routines and reconnect with the divine.

One of my favourite examples of a sacred pause is the ringing of church bells. In my previous parishes, the bells tolled regularly, their music filling the air and catching the attention of passers-by. I loved watching people stop, phones in their hands, to capture the resonant sounds.

While bell-ringing is a cherished tradition upheld by dedicated enthusiasts, its purpose extends beyond mere novelty. Historically, church bells served as a communal summons. Their chimes were more than just a call to service; they were an open invitation to pause daily labours and gather in worship and fellowship. The bells disrupted the ordinary, carving out space for the extraordinary.

Today, our pauses are often confined to weekends filled with leisure activities, errands or moments of respite. Even our holidays – originally 'holy days' – have shifted in purpose. Once, these periods were set aside for spiritual reflection, pilgrimages and deep reconnection with God. They were intentional breaks designed to interrupt the mundane with the sacred. Now, holidays often resemble brief escapes aimed at relaxation and diversion. They serve as intermissions from our responsibilities rather than opportunities to realign with our deeper purpose.

If we yearn to re-enchant our lives, to infuse them with meaning beyond the ordinary, we must reclaim these holy interruptions. Let's heed the call to reimagine our relationship with time and allow moments of sacred pause to be woven seamlessly into the fabric of our daily existence.

Place: from time as schedule to time as a place

When we think about time, we often imagine it as something that simply flows – a stream of moments that we move through, often without much thought. But what if we began to think of time as a place? A place where we can be truly present, rather than just another item on our schedule? This shift in perspective can be incredibly powerful, especially in prayer and spiritual practices.

We cannot teleport from one place to another physically, but with time, it is different. We can easily drift from one thought to another, jumping between worries, plans and distractions, and end up never really being where we intended to be. Thinking of time as a place grounds us, helping us to focus and be fully present in the moment, just as we are fully present in a physical space.

I have a friend who schedules a daily meeting with God, treating it just like any other important appointment – same time, same place. He turns up and is fully present. This practice underscores how viewing time as a place can transform our spiritual lives.

This concept is not new. In the Old Testament, time often became a kind of temple – a sacred space where people could encounter the divine. The Sabbath, especially when the Israelites were exiled and away from their physical land, became a temple in time – a consecrated period where they could reconnect with God, even if they could not go to the Temple in Jerusalem.[6]

For us today, seeing time as a place is a discipline. It makes the idea of retreat accessible, something we can do without needing to go on a physical pilgrimage. I have ministered in a variety of contexts, and I am aware of the different ways people live, but the opportunity to regard time as a place is open to all of us.

My old vicar would say to the staff team that a good start is to find an hour each day, a day each week, a weekend every month, and a month each year for renewal. These rhythms of rest and reflection are not just about managing our time. In these consecrated seasons – these places set apart for a specific purpose – our task is simple yet profound: to behold, to look at God and to allow God to look at us.

By thinking of time as a place, we can create a sanctuary in our daily lives – somewhere we are not merely passing through but in which we are fully present, intentional and connected with what truly matters.

Words: sacred space as a place to be held

The concept of a sacred space can feel intimidating. I have seen countless people approach the doors of our churches, peer through the windows and hesitate to enter, believing that they must have it all together to step inside. This hesitation reveals a common misconception: that one must be spiritually 'perfect' to enter a sacred space. However, these places are precisely where we are meant to come as we are, with all our flaws and doubts, to encounter the divine and to be transformed.

This truth became all the more real to me when I brought a priest friend to St Leonard's, the church where I first served as a priest. As we walked inside, he turned to me and said, 'Oh, I didn't realise it was a derelict building.' For a moment, I felt a pang of embarrassment. I quickly explained that while the roof had been repaired, we lacked the funds for further decoration.

Yet, the more I reflect on that space, the more I come to love it as it was. There seemed something profoundly right about imperfect people walking into an imperfect building – a place that let them know that they belonged. In other words, it felt almost poetic that the building was itself broken, for it spoke of a God who was broken for us, a God who welcomes broken people.

Looking back on my own journey, I recognise that sacred spaces, which I feel played a crucial role in nurturing my prayer life, were places where I could be fully present, where the walls seemed to absorb my thoughts, fears and hopes. In these spaces, the silence was more than just the absence of noise; it was the presence of God.

In the Anglican Church, we are fortunate to have churches in nearly every neighbourhood, and many of them are stunning. Yet sacred spaces do not have to be grand cathedrals or remote retreats; they can be simple, familiar places where you feel safe and at peace – a corner of your home, a park bench or even your car.

By creating or recognising a space like this in your life, you allow yourself to be held in God's presence, to encounter the divine in the middle of your daily life. These sacred spaces become a refuge where you can bring your whole self before God. Just as importantly, these spaces remind us that God is present wherever we open our hearts to him.

In a previous chapter of my life, I worked as a photographer. One day, I was covering Fashion Week in central London when, in the middle of the buzz, I was suddenly pushed aside by large men in black suits each wearing an earpiece. I was not the only one being elbowed aside; these security people were clearing a path, creating a sense of urgency and expectation.

Moments later, to my utter amazement, the Queen appeared! A mix of shock and awe rendered me speechless as she gracefully moved past, entered a lift and disappeared from view. The entire encounter was fleeting, yet it left a deep impression.

Reflecting on that moment, I realise how much more incredible it is that the King of kings, the Creator of everything, invites us to approach him. Unlike my brief and distant encounter with the Queen (she couldn't stop and talk to everyone), God eagerly desires to encounter us. The one who holds all power and authority welcomes us into his presence, inviting us to speak freely, to be heard and to be known.

Conversation with God reveals that prayer is the language of hope. I am reminded of the words of Nick Cave, a musician and writer known for his deep reflections on the human condition. On his website, Cave responded to a fan losing hope in the world with a profound statement: 'Hopefulness is not a neutral position either. It is adversarial. It is the warrior emotion that can lay waste to cynicism.'[7]

Making time for God, sitting quietly in a church or the sacred spaces we make in our homes, might seem like a simple act. But it is, in truth, a radical one. When we pray, we are not only seeking comfort; we are engaging in an act of defiance against despair. Prayer becomes a bold declaration that the world and its people are worth saving, and that our lives have meaning to the one who holds all things.

In the face of suffering and the valleys of death, prayer is our way of clinging to the promise that Jesus made: 'I am making everything new' (Revelation 21:5). It is in this trust, this steadfast belief that God's light will always break through, that hope finds its footing, grounding us in the radical grace of the kingdom of God.

Reflection questions

1 Have you ever found yourself in an unexpected place of prayer, somewhere where you have felt yourself either strongly in the presence of, or being held by God? What do you think sparked that connection in that place and time?
2 How do you find time to retreat and pray? How can you weave 'holy interruptions' into your day?
3 Where could become your 'safe place', somewhere where you can spend time being fully present to God and allowing him to be present to you?

© Madaliso Zgambo

Goodness Uwan-Owaji Victor is a multifaceted creative and poet of Nigerian heritage (Ijaw and Igbo) born and bred in North East London. Her work explores themes of faith, identity, personal history and racial justice.

She currently works within the music industry, creating opportunities for songwriters and producers and forging partnerships within the publishing industry.

Bible quotations in this chapter are taken from the ESV and Ikpa Mbuban the Bible in Obolo of Nigeria.

10

Good News, New Histories

For many young, Global Majority Christians, reconciling personal and collective faith with the Church's historical atrocities is deeply challenging work. Unsurprisingly, the complexities of the task are often swept under the carpet by believers from all walks of life, creeds and colours. However, contemporary racial tensions – as evidenced by the surge of race riots across the UK in 2024 – mean that it is ever more critical that our societies (and the Church) examine their role in addressing racial injustice.

My poem 'Good News, New Histories' is a brief exploration of these difficult themes.

> since we are
> surrounded
> by such a great
> cloud of witnesses,
> let us throw off everything
> that hinders and the sin
> that so easily entangles ...
>
> i reflect on
> a heavenly cloud of witnesses
> a multitude through

Good News, New Histories

the ages
cheering on
people of faith.

tainted hands, hardened hearts
and darkness hidden within.

i think of missionaries
well-intentioned,
ill-intentioned.
discord sown.
priests rejecting parishioners.
good news as lip service.

i think of those who profess they believe
humankind entwined with God,
imago dei,

yet refuse
to see
the image reflected
in faces
black or brown.

i think of the do-gooders,
blind eyes turned
away from their neighbour,
unwilling to ruffle feathers
in the ugly face of injustice.

Good News, New Histories

i've heard the 'thinkers' say,
'we cannot hold the sins of professing
Christians throughout the ages
against the Church.'

our shared histories
a mirror
speckled with
both good and evil.

how do we break bread
within the heart of darkness?
or find hope in unison?

maybe, when repentance truly abounds,
Good News,
New Histories
small glimpses of reconciliation.

now we are
surrounded
by such a great
cloud of witnesses,
let us throw off everything
that hinders and the sin
that so easily entangles …

eyi ogbogbo ebi ata-ikọ ewabe ikana eji ikeyi, eji esaña
otutuuk inu geelek òkigbugbana eji, mè ijo inu ya eyi

òkigwat lek igugobo eji ikam me ikafiatge mgbo, etop efiiñ, mè ekat ejit elibi ekot yi òkup eji me isi ililibi.
(*Iburu* 12:1)

Therefore, since we are surrounded by so great a cloud of witnesses, let us also lay aside every weight, and sin which clings so closely, and let us run with endurance the race that is set before us.
(Hebrews 12:1)

'Good News, New Histories' begins and ends with Hebrews 12:1, an image of true believers through the ages. It's a passage I found myself meditating on in 2019 during a visit to Elmina Castle, a slave trading post on the Cape Coast in southern Ghana. I was grieved to see a chapel in the centre of the grounds and Scripture engraved within its walls. It seemed such a stark image of historical wrongdoing. The question, 'Should those who worshipped on these grounds while committing such evil be considered brothers and sisters in Christ?' troubled me well beyond the trip. It would be easy to dismiss the people who attended the chapel as 'not Christians', but that does not remove them from the story of Christian faith.

My question still has no resolution, although it has sparked a continued analysis of what it means to be a Global Majority Christian in the modern age – and what racial justice within the Church context will look like fifty years from now.

'Good News, New Histories' closes with the same verse in both the ESV and my mother tongue, Obolo (spoken

Figure 1 Text from Psalm 132 above a door at Elmina Castle, Cape Coast, Ghana, 2019

Figure 2 St James' Parish Church, Ataba, Rivers State, Nigeria

by a small cluster of clans within the Niger Delta). This is a prompt to Western Christians, reminding them that people across the world engage with the Christian faith in many languages through their own cultural lenses. The passage reminds me of my great-grandmother, who was an Anglican convert. There are fond family stories of her waking up early to pray at her village parish church, and I often think of her among the great cloud of witnesses – a contrasting image to that of the parishioners of Elmina Castle.

There is hope to be found in the willingness of young, Global Majority people to engage in reflective and analytical work, as they hold in tension the evil of historical wrongdoings and the goodness and fruitfulness of the Christian faith. It is work to which we are all called.

Reflection question

How can we, as individuals and as the Church, address a legacy of racism while ensuring that such horrors are never repeated?

Bhanuka Warnasooriya is an ordinand in the Church of England. He came to the UK from Sri Lanka to join the Community of St Anselm. He then helped to lead the community for two years before moving to Cambridge to train for ordination.

Bhanuka is an organist and choral director who particularly enjoys a cappella and barbershop harmony. He has been a chaplain for the Church of England College of Bishops and is involved in ecumenical work and in advocating for Christian unity. As a young Christian leader, he hopes to become more engaged in the area of mental health and faith, and to research aspects of 'othering' in Christian circles.

Bible quotations in this chapter are taken from the NRSVUEA and the NIV.

11

A journey through a supper table

As humans, we love to plan things. Something in our DNA just makes us feel safer by being in control. As a planning freak myself, however, I'm all too conscious that things don't always go quite the way we imagine.

Let's take one of the simplest things we share in our common life together: a meal.

If you've had the great privilege of sitting down to eat with a family, you'll be aware of the potential for joy and chaos. Even with close friends, things can sometimes go pear-shaped. Jesus, in the gospel accounts of the many meals he shares, seems to be well aware of this. He had been planning one meal in particular for a long time.

Then came the day of Unleavened Bread, on which the Passover lamb had to be sacrificed. So Jesus sent Peter and John, saying, 'Go and prepare the Passover meal for us that we may eat it.' They asked him, 'Where do you want us to make preparations for it?' 'Listen,' he said to them, 'when you have entered the city, a man carrying a jar of water will meet you; follow him into the house he enters and say to the owner of the house, "The teacher asks you, 'Where is the guest room, where I may eat the Passover with my disciples?'" He will show you a large room upstairs, already furnished. Make preparations for us there.' So they went and found everything as he had told them; and they prepared the Passover meal.

When the hour came, he took his place at the table, and the apostles with him. He said to them, 'I have eagerly desired to eat this Passover with you before I suffer, for I tell you, I will not eat it until it is fulfilled in the kingdom of God.'
(Luke 22:7–16 NRVsuea)

At the heart of the gospels, we find Jesus creating community around him. I imagine that the Last Supper might have been attended not only by the apostles (who, not to put too fine a point on it, included stinky fishermen, money-hungry tax collectors and violent, zealous men) but also by some of the women who had followed Jesus from the beginning and even stayed until the end at the foot of the cross. We're talking about people from all structures of society with widely differing political views, who likely included those who hated or profoundly disagreed with one another, those who had dark pasts and those no one would even have thought of speaking to. That's the community Jesus seems to have created. Yet I don't believe that this is a scene where Jesus got the guest list wrong. Yes, it's a mess, but in a truly disconcerting manner, God invites us to sit and eat with him in the mess.

The Anglican Communion can seem similarly diverse and perplexing. We're a group of people from across the world, joined by history and (quite frankly) a messed-up journey, who probably wouldn't have chosen one another but seem to have fallen into the category of 'Anglican'.

As a Sri Lankan Anglican and an Anglican Sri Lankan, I used to think that the average Anglican was an English-speaking, middle-class white man. But the Anglican Church is actually present in 165 countries. Over eighty-five million Anglicans passionately worship God, and the average Anglican churchgoer today is a young, poor, black woman living in sub-Saharan Africa.[1] This might surprise you; I think that it would have shocked British missionaries from the 1800s even more.

It might seem as if the Anglican Communion is something that hasn't gone quite to plan. But is it? As we explore this, we could enter the choppy waters of history and the great schisms of the past and the present, but instead, I suggest that we journey through a supper table – a family meal – with its highs and lows. And as Henri Nouwen proposes in his book *Love, Henri: Letters on the Spiritual Life*,[2] let's go deeper into the words of the institution of the Eucharist, accepting Jesus' invitation to sit with him in the mess and eat with his friends.

> While they were eating, Jesus *took* a loaf of bread, and after *blessing* it he *broke* it, *gave* it to the disciples, and said, 'Take, eat; this is my body'.
> (Matthew 26:26, NRSVuea, my italics)

Reflection questions

1 Does making plans come naturally to you?
2 What do you feel when your work or life isn't going as you imagined?
3 How do you find hope when everything goes wrong?

Taken: Chosen or exploited?

***Jesus* took *a loaf of bread* ...** In Ephesians 3, Paul speaks about the mystery of the body of Christ and reveals a deep, radical truth about the Christian Church. It's a body we can *all* be part of, no matter the colour of our skin or the race or nation we belong to. It's tempting for us, in the twenty-first century, to feel rather complacent because we have such a good, socially important message (even if the Church doesn't always live up to it), but I think that the Jewish-majority early Christ followers would really have struggled to come to terms with this new identity. After all, the nation of Israel had been blessed in scripture as the chosen nation of God – God's own people – yet Paul is saying, 'There is neither Jew nor Gentile, neither slave nor free, nor is there male and female' (Galatians 3:28 NIV).

We'll return to this in a moment. For now, let's dwell on the bread Christ takes at the Last Supper. Whether our theology of the Eucharist is that Christ is really present in the bread and that it has turned into his body, or we believe that we're remembering Christ in the bread, the fact is that, through taking it in the presence of God, we offer ourselves to be taken as well.

A journey through a supper table

Yet unlike in the Last Supper where, surrounded by his friends, Christ *took* bread and so offered a grace to the world, the history of the Church is soaked in a different kind of *taking*: an abusive taking by European Christians of the humanness of those deemed lower than white-skinned beings. It's as if the former thought that they had been 'chosen' as a special race over others. As a Sri Lankan, I have seen and still live with the impact of colonisation in my nation and my church. The ugly animalising of those with darker skin tones, denigrating their lifestyle, culture and society, is a form of racism still present in the world – and the Church – today.

The Europeans who came to take and conquer the world didn't generally come with love and the spirit of the living God but rather with a sword and a Bible in their hands, using the latter as another (double-edged) sword to purify the 'dark' corners of the world with the light of Christ. This often resulted in forced conversions and 'holy' death threats. Selina Stone puts it like this:

> In the case of India, it was centuries after St Thomas is understood to have brought Christianity to that country that Europeans sought to enforce another version. Europeans arrived in 'dark' parts of the world, assuming that God was not there and that even if God had been there, global peoples needed Europeans to help them find God.[3]

Why are there so many Anglican churches across the globe? The answer is that they were founded as missionary settlements in the countries the colonisers settled in. The Church founded by the English in Sri Lanka (then Ceylon) would have been the Church of England in Ceylon, and is currently part of the Anglican Communion as the Church of Ceylon.

What's the impact of this, day to day, for Anglican Christians?

Well, a problem for me as a Sri Lankan living in the UK (though hardly, I concede, on a par with war and world hunger), is how long my name is. I have five names on my official documents, which means that whenever I'm asked to fill out a form, I run out of space almost immediately. My name makes clear that I come from a Sinhala Buddhist family tree, and I wonder whether, somewhere in my history, one of my ancestors was forcefully converted and baptised by those in thrall to status, education, money or power.

Everything that has been taken from me, my ancestors and many others across the globe by imperial rulers is a cause for lament for us as Anglicans, Christians and more deeply as humans. However, the Last Supper reminds us that Christ takes the bread, the bread is the body and the body is us. This image of being chosen is given to everyone, through the cross, and the dark origins of the Anglican Communion can't prevent us from receiving it. Our hope is therefore in the journey Christ is taking us on, and our joy is in the discovery that, when we truly believe that we are valuable in God's eyes, we recognise that others are valuable in his eyes too and that they have a place in his heart.

So, we being the bread that is *taken* (chosen), we are then *blessed* ...

Reflection questions

1 Do you find it hard to grapple with the understanding that Christ has taken (chosen) you?
2 How do you relate the taking done by colonial rulers to the taking of bread during the Last Supper by Christ?
3 What is the role of the Church as we look with hope towards a better future?

Blessed: Toxic positivity?

***Jesus* took *a loaf of bread, and after* blessing *it* ...** Saying grace at meals is just one of those things Christians tend to do – though for an interestingly varied length of time. There are those of us who start reasonably focused and then go on to thank everyone and everything in the food chain. At the other end of the spectrum (perhaps if we've been to boarding school), we might be content with a very short and sweet grace that scarcely lasts for two seconds.

This purpose of saying grace is to express our thanks for the provision of food and drink and to ask that it might be blessed. This is just what Jesus does at the Last Supper with the bread and wine. Earlier, I mentioned the promise God gave the people of Israel:

> I will make of you a great nation, and I will bless you, and make your name great so that you will be a blessing.
> (Genesis 12:2 NRSVuea)

The great nation that God has called his own was chosen, yes, but it was chosen to be a *blessing*. The blessing that came through the people of Israel was Christ, who through the cross has given us life everlasting. Being *taken* and then *blessed* is the continuous work of God in our lives and not a plan B.

Yet beautiful words and concepts can be purloined. Many of us will be aware of the popularity of feeling *#blessed* on social media (sometimes for rather phoney reasons). The reality is that the terminology of being blessed and feeling blessed has been overused, and its deeper meaning has been concealed. When we look at the world and the Church, it's very difficult to say that they're #blessed. Rather they seem to be *#cursed*.

I wonder if the Jewish people found it hard to feel chosen and blessed? The nation of Israel went through exile, slavery and abuse, and the Anglican Communion has gone through it too. How can the hope of a blessing be in sight?

To perceive the ultimate reality that we are indeed being blessed, we need to wait in prayer. We need to acknowledge our sins, our failures and our hurts. In some Christian circles, there can be a tendency towards toxic positivity, a propensity to dismiss any form of negativity and cover over the cracks with a 'God-is-always-good' bandage. But the Last Supper teaches us that the true Christian response to sin, negativity and struggle is hope. Hope is very different from optimism and positivity; hope is founded in faith. It doesn't ignore the elephant in the room but rather invites us to acknowledge and recognise suffering, though not to give it power. Hope invites us – and the whole of the Anglican Communion – to sit in the mess.

In 2022, I had the pleasure of being part of the chaplaincy team for the Lambeth Conference, which brings together the bishops of all dioceses that affiliate with the Anglican Communion across the globe. I vividly remember being in Canterbury Cathedral and gazing down at a mass of purple-clad, laughing, clamouring figures (surely the most unruly Christians ever!) It was such a wonderful sight that it brought me to tears. People from different nations, speaking different languages, who were black, white and brown, men and women, gay and straight, alongside those they loved and those they couldn't even think of loving, those they agreed with and those they didn't. They didn't ignore the pain around them, but sat with hope. A loud clatter filled this ancient mother church of Anglicanism, this house of God: a joyful noise before the Lord and an incarnation of John's vision:

> After this I looked, and there was a great multitude that no one could count, from every nation, from all tribes and peoples and languages, standing before the throne and before the Lamb, robed in white, with palm branches in their hands. They cried out in a loud voice, saying,
>
> 'Salvation belongs to our God who is seated on the throne, and to the Lamb!'
> (Revelation 7:9–10 NRSVUEA)

Amid pain, brokenness and suffering, we have a glimpse of the kingdom of God. Can you convince me that we are not blessed to be part of it?

We are *taken* and *blessed* to be *broken* ...

Reflection questions

1 To what extent do you feel blessed?
2 Do you feel that you have a tendency towards toxic positivity and, if so, why might this be?
3 Do you feel that the diversity of the Anglican Communion is a blessing we should celebrate more?

Broken: A pain-giving friend?

***Jesus* took *a loaf of bread, and after* blessing *it he* broke *it* ...** If you have siblings, you probably know how hard it is to share. 'He's got a bigger piece than me!' is something my mother would hear quite frequently as my older brother and I tussled at the supper table. Now I'm an adult, I miss those silly little fights – certainly, I wouldn't be the person I am today without all they contributed to my childhood.

Brokenness is part of the journey we're all on. The act of Jesus *breaking* the bread, taking it and blessing it has deep symbolism. We share the same food, the same joy and the same pain, though our brokenness reveals something unique about us. That's why we need to share it with our brothers and sisters. We are broken to be shared.

And maybe, just maybe, when we bring the broken pieces together, we will find something whole.

God is not afraid of our darkness and our brokenness. Christ is to be found as much in slums and war zones as in palaces and grand cathedrals. When thousands of children are perishing in bomb blasts, he is among them. When a mother is crying inconsolably for her dead son, Christ's own tears fall. When (whatever our apparent status in life) we are lonely or depressed, lost in the deep darkness of the Saturday between Good Friday and Easter Sunday, Christ is there, longing for resurrection with us.

The Anglican Communion is full of Spirit-filled disciples living out their faith, some in places of relative safety and some in places where people are not sure that they'll wake up the next day if they lay their heads down to sleep. One of my dear friends, my brother from South Sudan, told me:

> You know Bhanuka, I spent six years asking God why my mother and brothers were killed in front of me. The only answer God gave me for six years was silence, and then I met a young boy, whose family was killed in front of him just two days ago. And that young boy held my legs and started to cry. I know exactly how that boy feels, and so I just sat with him because I didn't have any answers. I cried with him and sat in silence. The silence lasted for more than three hours, and then suddenly this boy just started to sing, 'How Great Thou Art'. And that's when I knew the answer: God couldn't answer because he was crying with me.

We need to befriend our brokenness. It's only when we make friends with it that we move away from the curse of the 'why' – 'Why me?' 'Why us?' 'Why now?' It's so difficult to live without an answer to these 'whys' that we are easily persuaded to link events over which we have no control to our conscious or unconscious self-evaluation. When we have cursed ourselves, or allowed others to curse us, it's tempting to see our suffering as an expression or confirmation of that curse. But when we seek to find the face of God in the darkness, joy and pain become two sides of one desire: to grow and reach the fullness of the beloved of God. We are *taken* and *blessed* to be *broken*. Of the moment when God's plan seemed to have failed utterly and Christ's body was broken to pieces, Bishop Emma Ineson writes:

> We will never experience the same kind of failure that Jesus experienced on the cross, precisely because he was Christ and we are not. We will not experience separation from God because we are not the Messiah. We will also never experience separation from God precisely because of the cross. Because of the suffering Jesus experienced there, we will never be distant from God, no matter how bad our failure. There is always hope, always redemption – because of the cross, the ultimate symbol of failure.[4]

We who are taken, blessed and broken are seeking hope.

Reflection questions

1 What feels most broken in your life?
2 How do you respond when you see the brokenness of the world, the Church and ourselves?
3 Have you seen the face of Christ at a crucial moment in your life?

Given: Is it the final action?

Jesus* took *a loaf of bread, and after* blessing *it he* broke *it,* gave *it ... We have been on a journey through a supper table that changed the world and continues to change it still. Around the Lord's table, where everyone is welcome, earth and heaven unite as pain and brokenness are met by the reconciling love of God. This 'big bang' of transformation comes through a series of actions: taking, blessing, breaking and giving. And it has extraordinary consequences.

At the start of this chapter, I asked whether the Anglican Communion was something that hadn't gone quite to plan. My feeling is that it's a product of a failed and deeply flawed *human* plan (inhumane and racist), but I imagine that, in God's eyes, it's a much-loved part of his body – taken, blessed, broken and given – as he always intended. The Anglican Communion can define its nature as *giving*. The Spirit of God asks us to give the whole of ourselves and to lose ourselves to find God. In that process, we find ourselves afresh in God.

Yet, to be frank, this Christian definition of giving can seem more like *giving up* than anything else. I won't try to

A journey through a supper table

deny that, and I think that part of giving up is helpful to understand as self-emptying (*kenosis*).

Imagine for a minute what it might be like to surrender your plans for the day, the year, your church or even your life to benefit another brother or sister? This might seem inspiring, but it's pretty daunting, so let's return to the familiar idea of sitting down and having a meal. When we eat together, we're vulnerable to one another. Where there's an element of conflict, this might result in painful silences or shouting matches. On the other hand, a meal shared in peace and joy – notwithstanding our brokenness – is one of life's greatest moments. At such a meal, we're quite likely to encounter people – 'others' – we've never met before. Disconcerting perhaps, but we see in the resurrection narratives that Christ invites us to be full *givers* to strangers. This continuation of the supper meal in the upper room doesn't have a prepared guest list; rather *all* are invited.

It seems that the post-resurrection Christ actually looked like an 'other'. He was a stranger to even his closest friends. Most of the time, they didn't recognise him. It was only when they were fully willing to give all of themselves in vulnerable trust and faith that they perceived that he was the one they were longing for: the 'stranger' who emptied himself, left heaven and gave up his life for all humankind.

We, like his friends, are asked to give all of ourselves. That's when Christ becomes visible and hope is at hand. However, hope can best be described as a journey. As a person who suffers from severe depression, I know very well how difficult it is to find hope not only in the darkest moments but also in the brightest. What is bright to the world outside can still seem dark to one whose mind is not configuring the light. But that's exactly why I know how important it is to find hope every single day. It's my life support.

Hope is all we have, for me, for you, for the Church and for the world. Just hope.

I am reminded of one person who didn't have this life support of hope. Most of the disciples scrape through Holy Saturday to Easter Sunday, but one of my favourites couldn't give his all to Christ. I see more of myself in Judas Iscariot than in any of the other disciples. There's not a lot in scripture or tradition around Christ's work on Holy Saturday, but I find hope for Judas, and also for myself, through the simple yet deeply profound words of Ruth Etchells's 'The Ballad of the Judas Tree':

> In Hell there grew a Judas Tree
> Where Judas hanged and died,
> Because he could not bear to see
> His master crucified.
>
> Our Lord descended into Hell
> And found his Judas there,
> Forever hanging on the tree
> Grown from his own despair.
>
> So Jesus cut his Judas down
> And took him in his arm:

'It was for this I came,' he said,
'And not to do you harm.

My Father gave me twelve good men
And all of them I kept
Though one betrayed and one denied
Some fled and others slept.

In three days' time I must return
To make the others glad
But first I had to come to Hell
And share the death you had.

My Tree will grow in place of yours
Its roots lie here as well.
There is no final victory
Without this soul from Hell.'

So when we all condemn him
As of every traitor worst
Remember that of all his men
Our Lord forgave him first. [5]

God is shepherding our lives bit by bit so we can be open to being *taken*, *blessed*, *broken* and finally *given*. Our hope is in the same Spirit that hovered over the chaos in Genesis; the same Spirit that creates billions of universes; the same Spirit who breathes and gives life; the same Spirit who, through Mary, lifts the lowly high; the same Spirit that Jesus gave up on the cross for us; the same Spirit that overflowed on Pentecost. And this Spirit lives and breathes in you and me. The breath in our lungs is the breath of God, and it's through the slow and silent work of the Holy Spirit that we grow. If that isn't hope for the Anglican Communion and the world, I don't know what is.

Is giving the final action we need to perform to have hope? It looks like it. But in giving, someone takes, and the one who takes blesses, and breaks it and gives it again. Our Christian life – given in the abundance of the Spirit – is a meal that never ends.

Would you like to stay for supper?

Reflection questions

1 What do you think Christ is asking us to do as individuals, as the Anglican Communion, as a Church and as humans to restore hope in the world?
2 Can you think of moments when you have given everything you have but it still didn't seem like enough? What do you think Christ is telling you in moments like that?
3 Is hope enough?

Rachael Wooldridge is an associate vicar at Saint Paul's Hammersmith, having been on the clergy team at HTB. She is currently completing her PhD in Pauline Theology at Exeter University and teaches at St Mellitus College. She is married to Andy and is a mum to two small children.

Bible quotations in this chapter are taken from the NIV.

12

Hope in suffering

I recently sat in a coffee shop in Hammersmith chatting with a woman who has faithfully served in our church for some time. Being further along in the journey than me, she was asking about my hopes for my future, enquiring about where I saw my life going and encouraging me to dream big. I welled up.

Having hope has been something of a battle for me. There have been too many things that have not gone according to (what I thought was) 'The Plan'. The past few years have thrown more curveballs than I would ever have imagined possible, and my preference is not to think too much about the next few, let alone dream about them. If I've learned anything by the ripe old age of thirty-four, it's that life can be profoundly disappointing as well as beautiful.

What provoked me most during this conversation was the hope in the voice of my companion. Hope is the inevitable consequence of a life lived close to Jesus, and she radiated it. She knew parts of my story, and I was aware of hers, and I think that it's fair to say that neither has gone quite how we might have imagined.

I didn't grow up going to church, and although my parents both expressed faith of a sort, my dad was deeply suspicious of any institution that claimed to have a monopoly on God. He was convinced that if God was to be found, it would not be within the walls of a church. However, as a thirteen-year-old, I didn't initially attend to find 'God'; I went because of the promise of fast food after the Friday night youth group – and it didn't disappoint! Of all the evangelistic strategies churches engage with, they should really consider their use of fried chicken.

I might have been drawn in by the less-than-haute cuisine, but I stayed because of Jesus. I was fascinated by the stories I heard about him – what he taught, the life he lived and the death he died. It stirred a curiosity that I think exists in every one of us, a curiosity and a longing only truly satisfied when it encounters God's presence.

One Friday night, on the pale-green laminate floor of a church hall in the small East Midlands town of Scunthorpe, I sat and prayed a very simple prayer, giving my life to Jesus. A few months later, I was baptised, and there in the congregation, dosed up on painkillers and in a thick coat, was my mum. She had been in remission from cancer, but it had come back. This cold January morning was one of the first occasions she came to church with me, and it ended up being the last.

In the time up until Mum's passing, Dad had been alive with hope. Somewhere along the line, probably realising that it wasn't a reality he would be prepared to accept, the decision had been made not to reveal the true gravity of her prognosis to the two of us. I watched him, full of optimism, prepare for her chemotherapy and plan a family holiday to help her recover. And then, in what would become an all too vivid memory, I was startled awake by the sound of Dad shouting Mum's name. As I lay there, frozen and confused, he yelled for me. I ran into their bedroom to find him trying to resuscitate her, but she was no longer responding to his voice. He told me to call 999, and I ran out to the street to wait for the ambulance. The silence in the village that morning as I waited was deafening, and as the realisation of what was happening slowly began to overwhelm me, I found myself praying, 'Jesus, Jesus, Jesus.'

I think that Mum had had a vision of dying peacefully at home with us, but Dad hadn't got the memo. He refused to let her go on his watch. Instead, over the next few days, we watched her slip away on a steady stream of morphine surrounded by the bleeps of hospital machines. With her went more than I could possibly comprehend.

It's hard to put into the words the feeling of helplessness you experience in losing someone you love. The kind of pain you're left with leaves you extremely numb, with almost no capacity for anything else.

Of all the marks such an experience might leave on a fourteen-year-old, watching my dad fight so hard and with such hope only for that to earn him a seemingly greater heartbreak was one of the most profound. Over the next sixteen years, I watched as Dad too slipped away. The book of Proverbs says that, 'Hope deferred makes the heart sick' (Proverbs 13:12), and he became a walking illustration of this harsh truth. He had hoped for something more than he had ever hoped in his life, and it had not come to be. Over time, his grief became depression, and that depression forever changed our relationship. I've heard it said that time is a healer, but on its own, a healer it is not.

Hope in suffering

The subliminal message I picked up through my teens and twenties was that when the things you most hope for, most desire and most deeply long for do not happen, you quickly learn that hope can be dangerous. It's a lesson that's hard to unlearn.

I'll be honest and say that this wasn't an ideal start to me 'becoming a Christian'. I'm not sure that I would necessarily have responded to an invitation that said, 'Hey, give your life to Jesus and then watch your whole world blow up.' As much as I liked fried chicken on a Friday night, it wasn't worth this. Life as I had known it was gone. What was there instead, with the loss of my mum, was a deep crater, an unmissable landmark in my life, that seemed to speak only of a God who was absent. I'm sure that most of us have inhabited such places. The experience can leave us questioning our very belief in the existence of God, let alone a God who is loving and active.

In John 11, we read of Jesus walking into a village called Bethany, which literally translated means 'place of affliction', and he finds it thick with grief. The home of Jesus' friends Mary and Martha has recently become the resting place of their beloved brother Lazarus. We are told that Lazarus had been ill and that the sisters had sent a message to Jesus, presumably hoping that he would visit, answer their plea and heal their brother. This is the kind of thing that Jesus does. They had *seen* him do it. They knew that he *could* do it. Lazarus was his friend, and he loved him. Surely, he *would* do it. But Jesus doesn't seem to respond. He remains where he is for two more crucial days.

In the landscape of this village, Lazarus's tomb stands

as a monument to a God who is late. It speaks of Jesus' absence, of his inactivity, of an unanswered request. Unsurprisingly, when Jesus eventually arrives in Bethany, he is met by distress. Mary and Martha express the confusion and complaint that has been on many lips since: 'Jesus, if you had been here, this would not have happened' (see John 11:21, 32).

Here, we find the essential logic of one of the most challenging theological and philosophical questions of our existence: how do we reconcile the experience of human suffering with the existence of a loving God?

'If God was real, then surely this would not have happened.' It's relatively persuasive logic. I've heard it used perhaps more than any other argument as an objection to the Christian faith by everyone from adults in pubs to children in classrooms. It's a question as old as humankind, so it's no surprise to find it at the heart of what is widely thought to be the earliest book of the Bible and one of the most significant pieces of ancient wisdom literature still in existence: the book of Job.

It doesn't really matter if you view Job as a historical person or as a literary figure; what's important is that he is presented to us as the archetype of a righteous person, full of integrity and blessed by God. But Job suffers the loss of almost everything: his wealth, his children, his health and his social standing. The narrative explores the question we almost universally have when we witness suffering, the question I had in losing my mum and the question that lingers in the background of the tragedy that unfolds in Bethany in John 11: *Why?*

Job's three friends give us the answer. Eliphaz, Bildad and Zophar get a lot of flak for their below-par pastoral skills, and by the end of the story, we see why. But at least in their initial response, they are to be commended. Having undertaken a costly journey by travelling some distance to be with Job, they weep, lament and grieve with him. For seven days and seven nights, in the ashes of what was, they painfully, perhaps even awkwardly, accompany him in silence (see Job 2:11–13). This demonstrates what might have been – and in some cultures still is – a simple but natural response to suffering. It's not a practice we're particularly comfortable or familiar with in our culture (even, to be frank, within churches), but it's an essential part of the journey of grief in community. Sometimes, there are no words of comfort or practical solutions; there are only tears and lament, and we don't need to be afraid of this.

By day eight, however, sympathy and empathy have evaporated. Eliphaz, Bildad and Zophar turn to rationalising, justifying and trying to make sense of Job's suffering. There must be some fault, some reason, and they place the blame at Job's feet. This is a form of judgement, justice or discipline for Job's sin, they surmise. Viewing suffering as the result of sin is age old and still alive in Jesus' time (see John 9:2). No doubt, there is a type of suffering that is the result of sin, or one self-inflicted through free will. But Job teaches us that suffering is not a punishment, not earned, not deserved, not rational; rather it is the product of evil and a fallen world. Yes, God in his goodness is able to use what was intended for destruction and harm to create good. But evil, by its very definition, is chaos. It has no logic. It is the distortion and corruption of the true and the beautiful.

We read about how God rebukes Job's three friends because they have not spoken truthfully of God's nature in seeking to understand Job's suffering (see Job 42:7–9). God is neither its source nor its author. The book of Job, at its most basic, makes us aware that we live in a world where there are other forces at work, described to us through the language of Satan and sin. Jesus taught his followers to pray to our Father, 'Your kingdom come, your will be done,' precisely because we live in a world in which this is so frequently not the case. The logic of 'If God were real, this would not have happened' assumes that we live in a reality that perfectly aligns with God and his nature, but we do not.

So what answer does God give for Job's suffering? What is the reason, the rationale, the purpose behind everything Job has gone through? Outrageously, God does not give an answer at all.

The last few chapters of Job can feel like a hard read in some ways. Job's questions are met by a humbling monologue on the incomparable nature of God's power and majesty: 'I am God, and you are not.' If your hope in God is dependent upon all of life making sense, you will be disappointed. Job is reminded of his place in the world and of whose world it is. This requires a significant perspective shift, recognising that the 'why' question doesn't contain the answers we need.

The perspective shift doesn't end there. We realise that what is of most concern in the dramatic story of Job is not the tangible things Job possesses or loses, the kind of things our hearts and minds are mostly concerned with. No, to go back to the beginning of the story, we discover that what is at is stake is Job's very soul. Satan is not interested in Job's material circumstances, except in as much as they affect his relationship with God. Suffering is Satan's tactic for the demise of Job's trust in God. We think that the question driving the narrative is, 'Why is Job suffering?' But really, the question – after everything Satan has thrown at him – is, 'Will Job still trust in God?'

This is the question suffering poses to every believer in every season, stage and circumstance. *This* is the most urgent question we can contend with. The answer to this is directly connected to our capacity for hope. To go back to the account in John 11, it's this very question that Jesus poses to Martha in her hour of suffering too: 'I am the resurrection and the life … Do you believe in me?' (see John 11:25).

Will we believe in the *who* of God when we don't understand the *why* of our suffering, and when the reality of our circumstances painfully fails to align with the nature of God? This language of belief is the same as that of faith: *pistis*. But belief here is perhaps best interpreted with our understanding of the word 'trust'. So often, we read the idea of faith in the Bible as having faith for something, but really it's about having trust in someone. The language is subtle, but the consequences are profound. Too often, even in the name of Jesus, we can anchor our hope to a particular outcome in this life. But the Christian hope means trusting in God no matter the outcome. It's a trust anchored in the nature and character of God himself, not in and of this world.

At this point in my journey as a new Christian, as I wrestled with the 'why' questions of my mum's cancer, of the unanswered prayers for her healing, and of my dad's grief, I realised that it would be easier to be an atheist.

Not only would I get my Sunday mornings back (I've never been a morning person), but it would save me, surely, from having to contend with this level of theological conundrum? The emotional and spiritual tussle of figuring out how I felt about the God who had let this happen – to say nothing of the confusion about trusting or worshipping him – would stop. Indeed, that was my plan. No one had any answers for what had happened, so I figured that I had just been given what seemed like a cosmic 'get out of Christianity free' card, and I planned on playing it.

Little did I know that the simple prayer I had uttered only a few months earlier was about to wreak more havoc with my life than I ever could have imagined. Like the friend that only popped in for a cup of tea but is still there after dinner, God had been annoyingly present – and he didn't seem to be leaving any time soon. God does not evidence his love or his presence with us only through the answering of our questions or the explanations of life's unexpected twists and turns. God had, by this point, begun to litter my life with the evidence of his presence in other ways. He was like the stranger you keep seeing in the street. I had felt, amid the grief, the very thing I should not have logically felt: peace. From the car journeys back and forth to the hospital room with the beeps, to the funeral, to the late nights soaked in tears, I had felt a sensation that I can only describe as *like I was being held*, an awareness that he is God, and I am not.

I remember a moment when I sat on my bed planning my exit, and I sensed this question come back to me – the kind of nudge that I have since learned is the whisper of the Holy Spirit – *'Can you deny that I exist?'*

He called my bluff. As much as I wanted to, as much as it seemed to be the easiest option logically, as much as it seemed the simplest option emotionally, the option of denying God's existence with integrity was not open to me. God's silence to my 'why' questions had not equated to his absence in my life.

The question I was left with was, 'Could I trust him?' I had been taught not to trust strangers, but God was no longer a stranger. In just a short time, God had become a friend, one I couldn't deny or easily kick out of my life. But he was a friend I was mad at and confused by. My complaints, my tears and my anger became a sort of prayer, the only prayer I could really muster. Another nudge came: *'Revelation 7.'* Up until this point, I hadn't read anything of the book of Revelation – the pages of my new Bible were still stuck together at this place – so I was relieved to discover that there was a chapter 7 at all. With low expectations of what this 'end of the world' text might have to say to me, I read tentatively. It was a picture of a great multitude in white robes, of those who had gone through great suffering who were now before God, sheltered in his presence.

'Never again will they hunger;
  never again will they thirst.
The sun will not beat down on them',
  nor any scorching heat.
For the Lamb at the center of the throne
  will be their shepherd;
'he will lead them to springs of living water.'
  'And God will wipe away every tear from their eyes.'
(Revelation 7:16–17)

By the time I read the final verse, my Bible was wet with tears. Revelation, among other things, tells of the time to which all of history is heading, a time when all of reality will finally align with God's will and nature and when all contradictions will finally cease. No more cancer. No more depression. No more death. It speaks of the time when Job's accuser is finally silenced, along with his orchestra of sickness, evil and injustice. It speaks of the time, which we eagerly anticipate, as we will see in full bloom all that Jesus underwent and won for us on the cross. Fyodor Dostoyevsky describes this time poetically on the lips of Ivan in *The Brothers Karamazov*:

> I have a childlike conviction that the sufferings will be healed and smoothed over, that the whole offensive comedy of human contradictions will disappear like a pitiful mirage, a vile concoction of man's Euclidean mind, feeble and puny as an atom, and that ultimately, at the world's finale, in the moment of eternal harmony, there will occur and be revealed

something so precious that it will suffice for all hearts, to allay all indignation, to redeem all human villainy, all bloodshed; it will suffice not only to make forgiveness possible, but also to justify everything that has happened with men.[1]

I don't think that I quite appreciated at fourteen years old – and still don't think that I fully comprehend – the magnitude of what the Christian hope is ultimately set on, the horizon to which it reaches, or the scope that it encompasses, which profoundly changes our perspective of what is happening now, if we let it. But I had grasped that I had heard God speak to me, and it changed everything.

In the years after my mum's passing, my dad developed a perhaps understandable anxiety about his health, particularly when it came to cancer. There was a period of a few years where it became particularly consuming, where he had multiple trips to the doctor and multiple tests that would all come back confirming that he did not have cancer and he did not need to be worried. Then, shortly after my daughter's birth, in an unusually peaceful season of family life where our relationship seemed to be restored and more 'normal' than I would have thought possible, my dad got cancer.

It felt like a bit of a sick joke. My maternity leave was spent doing late-night car journeys between home in London and the hospital in Hull while my baby daughter slept blissfully unaware. We were back to the smell of hospital wards and the bleeps of machines, the cancer and the chemo, the fighting and the hoping. In that year, I experienced some of the most beautiful moments I had ever had with my dad, treasuring the simple joys of ice creams together and the light relief of Wimbledon on the television. And yet, in almost perfect parallel, it was one of the most painful seasons of my life. On 25 July 2020, he passed away just as I was preparing to be ordained.

It was another moment in life that at first glance could look like it only speaks of God's absence. But I have begun to learn that it is often paradoxically so, in the pit, in the tomb, in the places that seem to make no sense, God most profoundly meets us and reveals himself to us. I wish that there was space for me to list all the ways God spoke and moved in that season; all the moments that seemed orchestrated by heaven while I found myself back in the hell of cancer; how, like in Lazarus's tomb, even surrounded by the stench of death, Jesus made himself known as the God of life.

Back to Bethany, we see that Jesus doesn't respond to the death of Lazarus with answers, but he does respond with love. In John 11:35, the shortest verse in the Bible, we read that 'Jesus wept.' Jesus, the resurrection and the life, feels the pain of a world that is not how it should be. He grieves it, even though he knows what he's about to do. Jesus never negates the reality of people's sickness, sin or suffering and neither should we. But the problem with hope is that it means living in a contradiction. This moment at the tomb of Lazarus gives language to the tension we live in as Christians as we anticipate and trust in the life God offers despite the circumstances.

Hope in suffering

In a world filled with so much death, hope becomes a holy act of resistance that refuses to believe that this is how it was meant to be – or how it forever will be. But in this tension, we must, like Mary and Martha, say to Jesus, 'Come,' and invite him into the tombs and craters, and let him speak. They're not pretty, these places in our lives. 'They stinketh,' as the King James Version states. But these places of pain, disappointment and grief can, in his presence, become the very seedbeds in which hope grows.

As I walked away from the coffee shop that Tuesday afternoon, I was provoked by an old familiar question: will I trust God? Will I trust him not just with my past or my present but with my future? It had been a long season of learning to trust him in loss, in grief. But I felt him asking whether I would trust him not just in death but in life in this new season, and I wondered what he wanted to say to me about it all.

There's so much I don't know and still don't understand. But the Christian hope is not a naive hope. It doesn't grow in a greenhouse, sheltered from the painful realities of life. The Christian hope is a wild, evergreen hope that can't help but grow in our lives when Jesus is present, even in the craters and tombs. If my short journey so far has taught me anything, it is that this relationship with God – this journey of inviting him in and holding on to who he is and who he will be – is worth the battle. It's worth working through the frustrations and the anger, and of doing all the stages of grief *with* him. It's worth the pain of letting him in in order to hear his voice, the only voice that can bring dead things to life. Ultimately, this is the most important relationship we will ever have, because it is the only relationship that will outlive *everything* else, even death itself.

So I write to encourage you – in the middle of everything you might experience that contradicts God's loving nature – to take courage and hold on to hope. Trust that death does not have the final word, but Jesus does. And may you hear Jesus, in the darkness of whatever is going on in your world, calling you like he called Lazarus, by name, into life. A life without end.

Reflection questions

1 When you look back on the challenging seasons in your life, how and where can you see that God was present or at work? How did your relationship with God change that experience?
2 Read Revelation 21:1–8. Reflecting on this passage, how does this Christian expectation of a 'new heaven and a new earth' change your perspective on your current circumstances or what you've experienced?
3 Seasons of grief or suffering can feel deeply isolating. How can we come alongside people in those seasons? What is helpful, and what can be unhelpful?
4 Proverbs 3:12 says that, 'Hope deferred makes the heart sick.' Are there places where this has felt true for you? Take a moment to pray. Inviting the Holy Spirit, ask him to speak to you about this. Make this a regular conversation you have with God, perhaps journalling these times of prayer.

5 This chapter talked about the difference between having faith *for* something and having faith *in* someone. What does this difference look like in practice? What reasons does God give us to be able to trust him?

Notes

1 Seeds of unity: Alysia-Lara Ayonrinde

1 Harvey Kwiyani, *Multicultural Kingdom: Ethnic diversity, mission and the Church* (London: SCM Press, 2020), p. 5.
2 Olayinka Joseph, *Together Everyone Achieves More* (Houston TX: Indigo Riverbank Books, 2015).
3 Links to Professor Paul Miller's works can be found at 'Professor Paul W. Miller', *The Institute for Educational & Social Equality*, https://instituteforequity.ac.uk/professor-paul-w-miller/.

3 Kingdom, faiths and diplomacy: Cameron Howes

1 A full and comprehensive expounding of this image can be found in Rowan Williams, *Looking East in Winter: Contemporary thought and the Eastern Christian tradition* (London: Bloomsbury Continuum, 2021).
2 More information about the Faith Centre's approach and its activities can be found at 'Faith Centre', *The London School of Economics and Political Science*, https://info.lse.ac.uk/Current-Students/Faith-Centre.
3 Cameron Howes, 'Could Religious Dialogue be an Unexpected Antidote to Eschatological Anxiety?', *LSE Blogs*, November 17 2022, https://blogs.lse.ac.uk/religionglobalsociety/2022/11/could-interreligious-dialogue-be-an-unexpected-antidote-to-eschatological-anxiety/.
4 'The Future of World Religions: Population Growth

Projections 2010–2050', *Pew Research Center*, 2 April 2015, https://www.pewresearch.org/religion/2015/04/02/religious-projections-2010-2050/.

5 See James Walters, *Loving Your Neighbour in an Age of Religious Conflict: A new agenda for interfaith relations* (London: Jessica Kingsley, 2019).

6 Burhan Wazir, 'Finsbury Park Van Attack: Why an imam saved a terror suspect', *The Guardian*, 19 December 2017, https://www.theguardian.com/news/2017/dec/19/finsbury-park-van-attack-why-imam-mohammed-mahmoud-saved-terror-suspect.

7 More information on the Beecken Faith and Leadership Programme can be found at 'Beecken Faith and Leadership, *The London School of Economics and Political Science*, https://info.lse.ac.uk/current-students/Faith-Centre/Programmes/Beecken-Faith-and-Leadership.

8 David F. Ford, 'Scriptural Reasoning: Its Anglican origins, its development, practice and significance', in *Journal of Anglican Studies,* Volume 11, Issue 2, September 2013, pp. 147–165.

9 More information on the mission and activities of the Rose Castle Foundation can be found at 'A Global Network of Leaders Formed for Reconciliation', *Rose Castle Foundation*, https://www.rosecastlefoundation.org/.

10 More information on what scriptural reasoning is, how to do it, and some exemplary resources in the form of text packs and facilitation guidance can be found at 'Reflecting Together on Sacred Texts', *Scriptural Reasoning Rose Castle Foundation*, http://www.scripturalreasoning.org/index.html.

11 'British Council and London School of Economics Organizes Faith and Climate Workshop in Egypt', *Egypt Today*, 27 July 2023, https://www.egypttoday.com/Article/1/125895/British-Council-and-London-School-of-Economics-organizes-Faith-and. (Accessed 20 September 2024.)

12 James Walters and Hanane Benadi, 'Can Faith Groups Drive Action on Climate Change?' *LSE Blogs*, 30 October 2023, https://blogs.lse.ac.uk/religionglobalsociety/2023/10/can-faith-groups-drive-action-on-climate-change/.

13 Cameron Howes, 'Faith and Climate Change: Engaging religious communities in climate discourse', *Bond*, 3 November 2023, https://www.bond.org.uk/news/2023/11/faith-and-climate-change-engaging-religious-communities-in-climate-discourse/.

4 Wild paths of peace: Martha Jarvis

1 For facts about Mozambique and the gun amnesty, see Eric Morier-Genoud et al., *The War Within: New perspectives on the civil war in Mozambique, 1975–1992* (Rochester, NY: Boydell & Brewer, 2018) and 'Mozambique: The bishop who smashed guns at the altar', *All Africa*, https://allafrica.com/stories/201403211253.html.

2 Facts about the indigenous peoples of Australia can be found at 'Who are the stolen generations?' *Healing Foundation*, https://healingfoundation.org.au/resources/who-are-the-stolen-generations/ and 'Suicide & self-harm monitoring', *Australian Institute of Health and Welfare*, https://www.

aihw.gov.au/suicide-self-harm-monitoring/data/
populations-age-groups/suicide-indigenous-australians.

3 For further interpretation of Psalm 85, see John Paul
Lederach, *The Journey Toward Reconciliation* (Waterloo:
Herald Press, 1999), pp. 52–62. Lederach's dramatisation
of the Psalm, which is based on his experiences of
mediating in Nicaragua, is well worth reading in full.

Much of the language in this chapter is drawn from
the Difference course, a short course about everyday
peacemaking created by the Archbishop of Canterbury's
Reconciliation Ministry. It is a powerful way of
conceptualising the habits of peacemaking we see Jesus
practise, which we can apply to our lives day by day. More
information about the course can be found at 'Make Your
Faith Count in a Complex and Divided World', *Difference*,
https://difference.rln.global/.

Filmed versions of some of the stories in this chapter
were used as part of the Anglican bishops' preparations
for the Lambeth Conference and can be found at
'Ministry in a Conflicted World', *Lambeth Conference*,
https://www.lambethconference.org/phase-1/
ministry-in-a-conflicted-world.

5 Hope and the Church of England: Cathrine Fungai Ngangira

1 David Goodhew, 'The Church of England
After COVID: Quo Vadis?' in *Covenant*,
5 March 2024, https://livingchurch.org/covenant/
the-church-of-england-after-covid-quo-vadis/.

Notes

2 'From Lament to Action', *The Church of England*, https://www.churchofengland.org/sites/default/files/2021-04/FromLamentToAction-report.pdf.

3 'Trust and Trustworthiness Within the Church of England', *The Church of England*, https://www.churchofengland.org/sites/default/files/2024-06/gs-2354-trust-and-trustworthiness-within-the-church-of-england-a-preliminary-report.pdf. See also 'The Anglican Church: Safeguarding in the Church of England and the Church of Wales Investigation Report', *Independent Inquiry Child Sexual Abuse*, https://www.iicsa.org.uk/document/anglican-church-safeguarding-church-england-and-church-wales-investigation-report.html.

4 'What is the Church of England?', *The Church of England*, https://www.churchofengland.org/media/stories-and-features/what-church-england.

5 Josef Pieper, *On Hope* (San Francisco, CA: Ignatius Press, 1996).

6 See Jürgen Moltmann, *Theology of Hope: On the ground and the implications of a Christian eschatology* (Norwich: SCM Press, 2021).

6 A vision for hope in politics: Keziah Patterson

1 William Wilberforce wrote these lines in his diary in 1787.

2 'We Seek Your Kingdom' was commissioned by London Institute for Contemporary Christianity (LICC) and Thy Kingdom Come. Information and full lyrics can be found at '"We Seek Your Kingdom" song with LICC', *Thy Kingdom Come*, https://www.thykingdomcome.global/resources/we-seek-your-kingdom-song-licc.

Notes

3 'Boris Johnson Resignation: Sajid Javid says prayer meeting moved him to quit', *BBC News* 10 July 2022, https://www.bbc.co.uk/news/uk-politics-62113401#:~:text=England%27s%20former%20Health%20Secretary%2C%20Sajid,breakfast%20in%20Parliament%20on%20Tuesday .

4 Sajid Javid's Personal Statement can be read in full at 'Personal Statement: Volume 717 Debated on Wednesday 6 July 2022', *UK Parliament*, https://hansard.parliament.uk/commons/2022-07-06/debates/B38E3EE2-6911-474B-89F0-90301B621F34/PersonalStatement.

5 See Andy Flannagan, *Those Who Show Up* (Edinburgh: Muddy Pearl, 2015).

6 There has been much discussion in academic literature about how best to define populism. My own view and definition has been shaped by Cas Mudde. See, for example, Cas Mudde, 'The Populist Zeitgeist', *Government and Opposition*, Volume 39, Issue 4, 2004, pp. 541–563.

7 Widening horizons: Hannah Spiers

1 Rowan Williams, *Luminaries: Twenty lives that illuminate the Christian way* (London: SPCK, 2019), p. xiii.

2 See 'Chapter 6, Trust', *Rule of Life: The Community of St Anselm a year in God's time*, https://stanselm.org.uk/wp-content/themes/vu-theme/assets/images/RuleofLifeBooklet.pdf.

3 Coky Giedroyc, dir. 'The Nativity', BBC, 2010.

4 See Gastón Espinosa, *William J. Seymour and the Origins of Global Pentecostalism: A biography and documentary history* (Durham, NC: Duke University Press, 2014).

5 Dave De la Fuente, 'The Duty of Remembering Pentecost', *Daily Theology Blog*, 14 October 2020, https://dailytheology.org/2020/10/14/the-duty-of-remembering-pentecost/.

6 Jean Pierre de Caussade, *The Sacrament of the Present Moment* (San Francisco: Harper, 2009).

7 'The Spirituality of Charles de Foucauld', *St Martin in the Fields*, https://www.stmartin-in-the-fields.org/the-spirituality-of-charles-de-foucauld/.

8 C. S. Lewis, *The Screwtape Letters* (London: Macmillan, 1942), pp. 75–76.

9 From a prayer by St Teresa of Avila. See 'God Alone Suffices', https://www.oxfordreference.com/display/10.1093/acref/9780191826719.001.0001/q-oro-ed4-00010805.

10 See Sarah Coakley and Matthew Bullimore eds. *The Vowed Life: The promise and demand of baptism* (Norwich: Canterbury Press, 2023).

8 A beautiful and messy awakening: Belle Tindall

1 William Shatner, *Boldly Go: Reflections on a life of awe and wonder* (New York: Atria Books, 2022), pp. 89–90. Emphasis original.

2 He is far better at telling his story than I am. If you like, you can learn more about the mystical and magnificent Martin Shaw in his episode of my podcast. See 'Martin Shaw: Re-enchanting … Visions, Dreams

and Storytelling', *Seen and Unseen*, https://www.seenandunseen.com/martin-shaw-re-enchanting-visions-dreams-and-storytelling.

3 Thomas Lyons, 'When a Christian Revival Goes Viral', *The Atlantic*, https://www.theatlantic.com/ideas/archive/2023/02/asbury-kentucky-university-christian-revival/673176/ (accessed 31 October 2024).

4 This conversation took place as 'The God Debate' at the inaugural Dissident Dialogues Conference in New York. The transcript can be viewed at 'Richard Dawkins vs Ayaan Hirsi Ali: The God Debate', *Unheard*, https://unherd.com/watch-listen/the-god-debate/.

5 I didn't leave her hanging, we're still in touch and she's still trailing after those soul cravings of hers. Her explorations, both professional and personal, continue.

6 'I Still Haven't Found What I'm Looking For' Lyrics © Polygram Int. Music Publishing B.V.

7 C. Kavin Rowe, *World Upside Down: Reading Acts in the Graeco-Roman world* (Oxford: Oxford University Press, 2010), p. 34.

8 Chris Russell, *Yearning for the Vast and Endless Sea: The good news about the Good News,* (Norwich: Canterbury Press, 2024), p. 8.

9 The radical grace of God: Toby Thomas

1 This quote is originally from Owe Wikström, Professor in Psychology of Religion at The University of Uppsala. He was quoted in the epigraph of Susan Cain, *Bittersweet: How sorrow and longing make us whole* (Crown Publishing, 2022).

Notes

2 Ronald Rolheiser, *The Holy Longing* (New York, NY: Doubleday, 1999).

3 Jon Tyson, 'God Comes Where He's Wanted', Church of the City New York, https://www.youtube.com/watch?v=8W9BQAjQN8s (accessed 25 October 2024).

4 Strahan Coleman, *Beholding: Deepening our experience in God* (Colorado Springs, CO: David C. Cook, 2023), p. 36.

5 Coleman, *Beholding*, p. 40.

6 This idea was expressed by N. T. Wright in the 2019 St Hild Lecture. See 'Space, Time and History: Jesus and the challenge of God', *N. T Wright Page*, https://ntwrightpage.com/2019/04/14/space-time-and-history-jesus-and-the-challenge-of-god/.

7 'Issue 190, April 2022', *The Red Hand Files*, https://www.theredhandfiles.com/do-you-still-believe-in-us/.

11 A journey through a supper table: Bhanuka Warnasooriya

1 See Philip Jenkins, *The Next Christendom: The coming of global Christianity* (Oxford: Oxford University Press, 2002).

2 See Henri J. M. Nouwen, *Love, Henri: Letters on the spiritual life* (New York: Convergent Books, 2016).

3 Selina Stone, *Tarry Awhile: Wisdom from Black spirituality for people of faith* (London: SPCK, 2023), p. 16.

4 Emma Ineson, *Failure: What Jesus said about sin, mistakes and messing stuff up* (London: SPCK, 2022), p. 149.

5 Ruth Etchells, *A Rainbow-coloured Cross* (London: SPCK, 2007), p. 168–169.

Notes

12 Hope in suffering: Rachael Wooldridge

1 Fyodor Dostoevsky, *The Brothers Karamazov*, trans. Richard Pevear and Larissa Volokhonsky (London: Vintage, 1990), pp. 235–236.